1996

150 Ways

to Increase Intrinsic Motivation in the Classroom

RELATED TITLES OF INTEREST

Improving Social Competence: A Resource for Elementary School Teachers
Pam Campbell and Gary N. Siperstein
Order No. H37575
0-205-13757-1

101 Ways to Develop Student Self-Esteem and Responsibility
Jack Canfield and Frank Siccone
Order No. 68844
0-205-16884-1

One Hundred Ways to Enhance Self-Concept in the Classroom, Second Edition
Jack Canfield and Harold Clive Wells
Order No. H54158
0-205-15415-8 (paper)
H57110
0-205-15711-4 (cloth)

Self-Talk for Teachers and Students: Metacognitive Strategies for Personal Classroom Use
Brenda H. Manning and Beverly D. Payne
Order No. H59488
0-205-15948-6

The Complete Guide to Learning Through Community Service: Grades K-9
Lillian S. Stephens
Order No. H51329
0-205-15132-9

Motivation to Learn: From Theory to Practice, Second Edition
Deborah J. Stipek
Order No. H46972
0-205-14697-X

Winners Without Losers: Structures and Strategies for Increasing Student Motivation to Learn
James P. Raffini
Order No. H40082
0-205-16707-1

150 Ways

to Increase
Intrinsic Motivation
in the Classroom

James P. Raffini

University of Wisconsin-Whitewater

Allyn and Bacon

Boston   London   Toronto   Sydney   Tokyo   Singapore

Library of Congress Cataloging-in-Publication Data

Raffini, James P.
  150 Ways to increase intrinsic motivation in the classroom / by
James P. Raffini.
    p.   cm.
  Includes bibliographical references (p.) and index.
  ISBN 0-205-16566-4 (cloth). — ISBN 0-205-16567-2 (pbk.)
  1. Motivation in education.   2. Classroom management.   I. Title.
LB1065.R316   1996
370.15'4—dc20   95-18933
                                                          CIP

Printed in the United States of America
10 9 8 7 6 5 4 3 2 1 99 98 97 96 95

CONTENTS

Preface ix

Chapter One

Introduction   1

Intrinsic Motivation   3
The Need for Autonomy
The Need for Competence
The Need for Belonging and Relatedness
The Need for Self-Esteem
The Need for Involvement and Enjoyment

TARGET Structures   12
Task Structure (T)
Authority Structure (A)
Reward Structure (R)
Grouping Structure (G)
Evaluation Structure (E)
Time Structure (T)

Chapter Two

Strategies for Enhancing Student Autonomy   17

Recommendations for Enhancing Student Autonomy   17
Strategy 2.1: Round Tuits
Strategy 2.2: Newsroom
Strategy 2.3: Goal Cards
Strategy 2.4: Floating A
Strategy 2.5: Quality Checklist
Strategy 2.6: Pick Your Points
Strategy 2.7: Check It Out
Strategy 2.8: Self-Awareness and Career Choice
Strategy 2.9: Goal Books
Strategy 2.10: Kid Questions
Strategy 2.11: Sentence Polishing
Strategy 2.12: Self-Report Card
Strategy 2.13: Social Studies Hot Seat
Strategy 2.14: Advanced Organizer
Strategy 2.15: Peacemakers
Strategy 2.16: Wellness Awareness

Strategy 2.17: Feelings Chart
Strategy 2.18: Coaching Choices
Strategy 2.19: Voting with Your Feet
Strategy 2.20: Teacher-Advisor Program

Chapter Three

Strategies for Enhancing Competence in All Students   68
Recommendations for Enhancing Competence for All Students   68
Strategy 3.1: Know-Want-Learned Listing
Strategy 3.2: The Unwritten Dialogue
Strategy 3.3: Estimating Esquire
Strategy 3.4: Graphic Note Taking
Strategy 3.5: Reflective Participation for Everyone
Strategy 3.6: Choral Poetry
Strategy 3.7: Math Mind Reading
Strategy 3.8: Crossnumber Puzzle
Strategy 3.9: Seeing with the Mind's Eye
Strategy 3.10: The Teaching Assistant
Strategy 3.11: Success Contract
Strategy 3.12: Word Sort
Strategy 3.13: Synectics
Strategy 3.14: Daily Math Journal
Strategy 3.15: Fit My Category
Strategy 3.16: Eliminating Failure
Strategy 3.17: Grading Rubrics
Strategy 3.18: The "I Can" Can
Strategy 3.19: The Death of "I Can't"
Strategy 3.20: The One-Hour Book

Chapter Four

Strategies for Increasing Belonging and Relatedness   121
Recommendations for Building Student Relatedness   121
Strategy 4.1: Cooperation Dilemma
Strategy 4.2: Measuring the Motivational Climate
Strategy 4.3: Appreciation Web
Strategy 4.4: Brainstorming Bonanza
Strategy 4.5: Nuts and Bolts
Strategy 4.6: Random Grouping
Strategy 4.7: Icebreakers
Strategy 4.8: Big and Little Buddies
Strategy 4.9: *Tropical Tribune*
Strategy 4.10: Five Squares
Strategy 4.11: Assertive, Aggressive, or Passive?
Strategy 4.12: Gumdrop Tower
Strategy 4.13: Group Filmstrips
Strategy 4.14: Pinwheels
Strategy 4.15: Infomasters

Strategy 4.16: Multicultural Celebrations
Strategy 4.17: Can You Top This?
Strategy 4.18: Stranded
Strategy 4.19: Class Photo Album
Strategy 4.20: Super Squares

Chapter Five

Strategies for Enhancing Student Self-Esteem 181

Recommendations for Increasing Student Self-Esteem in the Classroom 181

Strategy 5.1: 3-D Self-Portrait Box
Strategy 5.2: Ugly Ducklings
Strategy 5.3: Put-Ups
Strategy 5.4: Name Bugs
Strategy 5.5: Life Line
Strategy 5.6: Similarity Wheels
Strategy 5.7: My Me Book
Strategy 5.8: Stick-On Encouragers
Strategy 5.9: The Day You Were Born
Strategy 5.10: Through the Gender Looking Glass
Strategy 5.11: Random Acts of Kindness
Strategy 5.12: The Gender Journey
Strategy 5.13: Silent Solutions
Strategy 5.14: Care Cards
Strategy 5.15: Resident Specialists
Strategy 5.16: Name and Body Acrostic
Strategy 5.17: Who's Like Me?
Strategy 5.18: Wanted Posters
Strategy 5.19: Family Book
Strategy 5.20: Accomplishment and Goal Sheet

Chapter Six

Strategies for Stimulating Student Involvement and Enjoyment with Learning 231

Recommendations for Stimulating Student Interest and Enjoyment 232

Strategy 6.1: Switch Day
Strategy 6.2: Function Machine
Strategy 6.3: Rhythm Pizza
Strategy 6.4: Animal Fact or Fiction
Strategy 6.5: Orienteering
Strategy 6.6: Anticipation Guide
Strategy 6.7: Know the Author
Strategy 6.8: Curious Questions
Strategy 6.9: What's the Score?
Strategy 6.10: Expanding a Model
Strategy 6.11: The Farmer's Dilemma
Strategy 6.12: Wordsplash
Strategy 6.13: Roundtable Rap

Strategy 6.14: "15"
Strategy 6.15: Pen Pal Picnic
Strategy 6.16: Going Fishing
Strategy 6.17: The Human Adding Machine
Strategy 6.18: Talking Chips
Strategy 6.19: Popcornology
Strategy 6.20: Floor Puzzles

References 281
Index 285

PREFACE

Former Secretary of Education Terrell Bell once remarked, "There are three things to remember about education. The first is motivation. The second is motivation. The third is motivation." This book has one primary purpose: To provide both elementary and secondary teachers with practical methods for dealing with this overwhelming concern.

For many teachers, the inability to directly control student motivation leads to feelings of frustration and helplessness. Some are tempted to invoke the old adage, "You can lead a horse to water, but you can't make him drink," when confronting the problem. Others rely on threats of punishment or bribes to motivate student learning in their classrooms.

Most students, however, resent being controlled by teachers. Some will confront teachers with statements like, "You can't make me do this," while others will rely on apathy or noninvolvement to assert their independence. Still others will complete the bare minimum to earn their rewards or avoid punishment.

Yet teachers are not powerless to influence student motivation. While we can't *make* horses drink, we can increase the likelihood of their drinking if we feed them a pail of salt before bringing them to the trough. Teachers can have a powerful influence over the intrinsic motivation of their students by arranging conditions in their classrooms that help students meet their psychoacademic needs for *autonomy, competence, relatedness, self-esteem,* and *enjoyment.*

Rather than salt, this book provides teachers with fifty research-based recommendations and one hundred teacher-tested instructional strategies for helping students experience intrinsic satisfaction from learning. These motivational strategies are in addition to the fifty strategies presented by the author in *Winners Without Losers: Structures and Strategies for Increasing Student Motivation to Learn,* published by Allyn and Bacon in 1993.

In *Winners Without Losers,* the author also provided an extensive, research-based discussion of how traditional educational practices can contribute to the structural causes of student apathy. The book also offered many classroom changes that can help overcome these structural problems. This book avoids duplicating that discussion. Instead, it provides teachers with a cornucopia of practical activities and suggestions for increasing intrinsic motivation in the classroom.

The ideas contained in this book are the result of the contributions of many people. I would like to especially thank the many teachers who, as graduate students, shared their beliefs and observations and worked together to develop strategies for meeting the psychoacademic needs of the students. I have tried to give credit to these who have suggested various strategies, and I apologize if I have missed anyone.

CHAPTER ONE

Introduction

Rewards and punishments are too often the only tools available in the motivational arsenal of many teachers. Although these two timeworn tactics can control many student behaviors, their indiscriminate use can seriously undermine students' intrinsic motivation for the activities and behaviors being controlled. Students will learn for many reasons. But the more their learning is manipulated by rewards and punishments, the less they will internalize what is being learned. We can coerce students into memorizing their spelling lists with gold stars or a threat of staying after school, but their attention will be focused on earning the stars or avoiding the punishment, rather than learning the value and benefits of this activity.

When pizzas, for example, are used to bribe a student to read, the purpose of reading is shifted and cheapened and the student's sense of self-determination in regard to reading is subverted. Making pizza contingent on reading tells young readers that a primary purpose for reading books is to obtain free pizza. Does the program work? Of course it works. It motivates students to read to earn pizzas. But, unfortunately, while parents and educators may be enticed by these short-term benefits, their long-term effects may be far more costly than the price of a few pizzas. According to psychologist John Nicholls, the long-term consequence of this program is likely to be "a lot of fat kids who don't like to read" (Kohn, 1991, p. 84).

If a pizza restaurant chain truly wants to foster an intrinsic love of reading in young children, its goal would be better served by reversing the reading and pizza variables—rather than making *pizza* the reward for reading, they should make *reading* the reward for pizza. For every pizza that students eat, for example, they would earn a certificate good for one free book at their local bookstore. In this case, it's reading that is valued, not the pizza. In their quest to obtain free pizzas under the current program, many young readers are being needlessly tempted to forego the intrinsic pleasures and challenges of reading to maximize their payoff by selecting the shortest and simplest books available.

There are more than one hundred research studies that demonstrate how external rewards and punishments can undermine the intrinsic motivation for many activities. For a complete discussion and review of this data see Lepper and Greene (1978); Deci and Ryan (1985); Kohn, (1993); and Raffini (1993).

The following scenario provides a simple dramatization of this process:

There was once a wise professor who retired from teaching to spend his remaining days savoring the tranquil music of the classical composers. His modest home bordered a quiet park, and there he enjoyed whiling away his days listening to his music and watching the seasons change outside his windows. One warm spring day, as the sounds of Mozart flooded his home, a group of teenagers appeared in the park nearby. They spent the morning talking and laughing while the speakers of their oversized tape player blasted the piercing shrills of a rock singer. Although the professor turned up the volume of his music and closed all of his doors and windows, he couldn't prevent the clamor from overwhelming the delicate strains of Mozart.

After the pandemonium had persisted for several days, the psychologist decided he would try to modify the behavior of the noisy teenagers. He considered several options: (1) he could ask the teenagers to move to another part of the park; (2) he could purchase larger speakers and try to blast out his adversaries with Beethoven; (3) he could reprimand the group for being so noisy and threaten to call the police; or (4) he could offer to pay each teenager a dollar if they would leave and never return.

Wise and experienced, the psychologist knew that all four options were fraught with problems. Although he relished the idea of pitting Beethoven against heavy metal, he recognized that approach could lead to his own citation for disturbing the peace. He also knew that requests were often perceived as orders and therefore easily denied; that threats usually escalate power struggles; and that paying teenagers to stop a behavior only increases the chances of it starting again—often by others looking for the same reward. Therefore, he chose a fifth option.

The next morning, a Monday, the group continued the ruckus. But when they were ready to leave the park, the old man came out of his house and told them that he loved hearing their music and laughter (years of psychological research had taught him that deception was sometimes necessary for the sake of science). If they would come back again tomorrow, he said, he would give each of them a dollar. Intrigued with the prospect of easy money, the group readily consented. Tuesday morning, they carried on as agreed and happily took his dollar in payment. The psychologist asked them to return on Wednesday, but this time he offered to give each of them only 50 cents. The adolescents agreed and returned the next day, whereon the psychologist promptly reduced Thursday's payment to a quarter. Reluctantly, the teenagers agreed. Finally, on Thursday, the psychologist gave each boy his quarter and said that he could no longer afford to pay them. Huffily, the teenagers said that they were not going to make their noise and play their music for nothing—and the wise old psychologist never saw the group again. (Raffini, 1993, pp. 63–64)

As previously cited, the research and theoretical analysis of the effects of rewards and punishments on student motivation have been reviewed elsewhere. The purpose of this book is to provide teachers with practical alternatives to punishment and bribery for increasing student interest and intrinsic motivation to learn. To understand the structure of these alternatives, it is necessary to examine the nature of intrinsic motivation.

INTRINSIC MOTIVATION

Intrinsic motivation is choosing to do an activity for no compelling reason, beyond the satisfaction derived from the activity itself—it's what motivates us to do something when we *don't have to* do anything. Many psychologists believe that humans are intrinsically motivated to seek out and to master challenges. This is particularly evident in young children when they are unencumbered by the restraints or expectations of others. When encountering a challenge such as getting out of a crib, opening a door, or tying a shoelace, they will often spend hours attempting to conquer it. The task, of course, must be within their capability. If it is too difficult, they will either cry in frustration, ask for help, or drop it until they have developed the skills necessary to master it. If the task is too easy, they will soon abandon it in favor of more difficult challenges. Rarely does one hear parents complain that their preschooler is "unmotivated" to learn.

The desire to seek and to conquer challenges is at the core of intrinsic motivation in the classroom. It is fueled by students' psychoacademic needs to control their own decisions (*autonomy*); to do things that help them feel successful (*competence*); to feel part of something larger than themselves (*belonging and relatedness*); to feel good about who they are (*self-esteem*); and to find pleasure in what they do (*involvement and stimulation*).

The Need for Autonomy

self select topics

Individuals seek a quality of human functioning that has at its core the desire to determine their own behavior; they have an innate need to feel

3

autonomous and to have control over their lives. This need for self-determination is satisfied when individuals are free to behave of their own volition—to engage in activities because they want to, not because they have to. At its core is the freedom to choose and to have choices, rather than being forced or coerced to behave according to the desires of another.

In the classroom, teachers often try to control students' behavior with rewards or punishments. Although these two techniques may be quite effective for influencing and controlling student learning and behavior, they usually stifle self-determination. The famous Swiss psychologist Jean Piaget believed that adults undermine the development of autonomy in children when they rely on the use of rewards and punishments to influence a child's behavior. Punishment, according to Piaget, is an externally controlled behavior management technique that often leads to blind conformity, deceit, or revolt in those being controlled. Children who choose to become conformists need not make decisions; all they need do is obey. Other children practice deceit to avoid punishment. When parents or teachers say, "Don't let me catch you doing that again!" children respond by exerting every effort not to get caught. Despite these accommodations to the reward-punishment system, children's need for autonomy usually resurfaces as they begin to revolt against the conformity pressures of punishment.

The use of logical consequences, rather than punishment, can encourage students to examine other viewpoints of their inappropriate behavior. Through dialogue with a teacher, students can focus on the tangible effects and natural consequences of their behavior. [Discussions of the differences between logical consequences and punishment can be found in Albert (1990), Dreikurs, Grunwald, & Pepper (1982) and Raffini (1980).] The use of external rewards to control behavior can also undermine self-determination and the need for autonomy. When students lose their sense of self-determination in the classroom, they relinquish control over what, how, and when behavior is to be performed.

Clearly, babies are born heteronomous and require the constant care, supervision, and control of an adult. Yet they also have an insatiable curiosity about the objects around them, grasping everything in reach, shaking, smelling, chewing, and then throwing it aside in favor of a new item. It is during toddlerhood, about age 18 months to three years, that children begin to strongly affirm their desire for autonomy and want to declare their independence from the constant control of adults. When parents are firm, yet reasonable, and do not overreact to these demands, children will begin to feel confident in themselves and will exercise self-control over their behavior.

With the onset of adolescence, students again begin to assert their need for self-determination. As they begin to define their own sense of

4

identity, they find it increasingly more difficult to accept adult direction. The more insistent teachers are with imposing their will and decisions on these young adults, the more they resist. Many conflicts between teachers and students have started with the statement, "You can't order me around and tell me what to do!" followed immediately with an "Oh yes, I can!" reply. Accepting adolescents' need for autonomy is the first step in helping them learn to assume the responsibility and consequences of their own behavior. Their desire to explore independently, undertake challenges, and solve problems provides the foundation for intrinsically motivated behavior.

Students' satisfaction of their need for autonomy is primarily a matter of gaining power and control over their lives. This process suggests that all students have a natural resistance to orders like "Sit down"; "Get out your books"; "Pay attention"; "Do problems 1 through 10"; or "Stop teasing the gerbil." Some students, recognizing the purpose of these commands, suppress the desire to resist and choose to conform. Others, who may also agree that the orders are necessary, bristle at the thought of being controlled by others; they often assert their desire for autonomy by resisting. One need only watch television in a room where another person controls the remote channel changer to experience the acute frustration of being controlled by others.

Chapter 2 offers ten recommendations and twenty specific motivational strategies that teachers can use to help all students develop and maintain a sense of autonomy and self-determination in the classroom.

The Need for Competence

In addition to the need for autonomy, individuals have a need to feel successful in their attempts to understand and master their environment. This need for competence motivates people to behave in ways that allow them to feel capable and effective.

This assertion seems to contradict many behaviors observed in students in middle and high school classrooms. How can we ascribe a need for competence to Eric, for example, who has been absent from his English class twenty-two times this quarter, or to Leslie, who hasn't completed a single math homework assignment in four weeks? Although these are difficult questions to answer, it is important to affirm that students do not choose ignorance over competence when all factors are equal. Furthermore, it is usually the desire to protect a fragile sense of self-worth that prompts unsuccessful students to choose apathy over involvement; they believe that they will experience less threat to their self-esteem if they withhold effort than if they were to expend effort and not be capable of experiencing success. After repeatedly pounding one's head against a wall, it feels good to stop—even when others encourage you to continue pounding.

Robert White was one of the first psychologists to assert that all human beings have an innate need for competence (1959). His definition of competence referred to the broad desire of individuals to interact effectively with their environment. He believed this desire for mastery provided the driving force behind behaviors designed to explore, understand, and conquer one's surroundings. Effectance behaviors, as White called them, range from the irresistible impulse of infants to grasp and then transport to their mouth almost any object within reach, to the focused intensity of teachers who become so absorbed in preparing an instructional unit that they lose track of time, disregard other obligations, and occasionally forget the needs of their families. The desire for competence is sometimes so intense that people will often persist in activities even when they may be difficult and painful. Young children do not stop trying to walk because they fall, nor do adults stop struggling to grasp an unfamiliar idea because it is complex and challenging.

Harnessing the natural energy of a student's need for competence and channeling it into the achievement of classroom goals is one of the biggest challenges faced by teachers. It seems almost impossible to orchestrate an environment in which twenty to thirty-five individuals have the opportunity to pursue their personal and unique definitions of competence. Yet if teachers are to persuade students to voluntarily do what is required of them, then enlisting their intrinsic need for competence can be a beneficial step toward that end.

The more students feel successful when performing an activity, the more intrinsically motivated they will be to persist in that activity. This assumes, of course, that performance of the activity occurs within a context that provides for self-determination, and that the requirements of the activity provide the student with a continued challenge. If, for example, the student acquires a skill to the point that increased mastery is no longer evident or possible, he or she will consider dropping the activity in favor of one that provides a new challenge. This is particularly evident in the discouragement experienced by musicians or athletes when they reach a seemingly insurmountable plateau in their skill level. Differences in student learning rates make the task of providing challenges to students a challenge for the teacher. Yet there is considerable research to show that when students are free to choose an activity, most will select one that provides them with a moderate challenge. However, students who have had a history of failure in school or are deprived of a sense of competence after persistent and repeated efforts toward mastery of an activity are likely to avoid contact with the activity in the future or, when contact is unavoidable, withhold effort toward learning. One need only observe the sets of golf clubs or tennis rackets abandoned in the corners of basements or attics to appreciate the feelings of success or improvement necessary to maintain an intrinsically motivating activity.

Appreciating the importance of the needs for competence and self-determination is crucial to increasing intrinsic motivation in the classroom. Observing a twelve-year-old manipulate a Mario brother through a computer-generated Nintendo maze clearly demonstrates the persistence and energy generated by a desire for a sense of competence. The complex programs in these computer games provide an almost limitless progression of challenges for players at all skill levels; novices and experts can spend hours totally absorbed in these challenges as their proficiency improves.

Although parents often restrict the time children spend playing these games, rarely do they insist or require children to play them. When given the freedom to play, children typically have control over what games to choose and how long to continue them. However, as the wise old psychologist clearly knew, one's sense of autonomy can be influenced and manipulated by others.

Chapter 3 offers ten recommendations and twenty specific motivational strategies that teachers can use to help all students develop a sense of competence in the classroom.

The Need for Belonging and Relatedness

The need to belong and to relate to others has a significant influence on a student's intrinsic motivation in the classroom. Having one's being recognized and accepted by peers is a psychological need of all students. Furthermore, achievement is enhanced when friendships within the classroom are broadly dispersed and when students are willing to help and support one another. In many classrooms, a student's "lack of motivation" can be traced to a real or imagined fear of being isolated or rejected by peers and being labeled a "brain," "nerd," or "retard," or derided for "acting white."

Adlerian psychology can be useful for understanding and reducing these fears. It is founded on the principle that human behavior is embedded in a social context, and the need to develop a sense of social and psychological belonging is a major challenge of childhood. Adlerians used the term "social interest" to represent an individual's capacity to develop a sense of belongingness with humankind and a willingness of the individual to contribute to the common good. Rudolph Dreikurs, the founder of American Adlerian psychology, believed that all humans were social beings with a basic desire to belong to a group. Indeed, Dreikurs believed that there may be nothing more painful while growing up than feeling isolated, rejected, and alone (1968).

Dreikurs also believed that since children grow up in a world of giant adults, they all experience feelings of social inferiority. Many students overcome these feelings as they become accepted and valued in their own right by parents, peers, and teachers. Such acceptance builds a base of personal security and confidence in their social position, and it provides students with the strength they need to unite with others for their mutual benefit. Other students are not so fortunate. Continued comparisons with brothers, sisters, and classmates add to their sense of social inferiority and force them to discover ways to compensate for these feelings, or to withdraw from social participation.

Some individuals try to compensate for inferiority feelings by striving for self-elevation, or a sense they they are better than others. Our competitive society seems to encourage this vertical striving, but the risk of such behavior is the loss of an even broader sense of social belongingness and security. Others forsake such competitive striving and give way to their feelings of hopelessness and despair.

Dreikurs warned that child rearing was particularly difficult in democratic societies where bribes, threats, rewards, and punishments are often diametrically opposed to the democratic goals of equality and a freedom of choice. Although it may not be apparent in many homes and classrooms, democracy requires that we treat all children and students with an equal measure of respect—a respect that Dreikurs believed is undermined when parents and teachers repeatedly impose their personal power over children (Dreikurs & Soltz, 1964).

When students from a variety of economic, racial, and social backgrounds come together in the classroom, each is highly motivated to secure a place within the group. Many develop a sense of belonging and acceptance by conforming to the social and academic expectations of their teacher and peers and by making useful contributions to the group's solidarity. Others become discouraged by their attempts to gain acceptance. Being unsuccessful with what they perceive to be constructive means for obtaining social belonging, they are forced to seek alternative, antisocial methods for gaining status. The class clown, the angry and defiant rebel, the vicious bully, the hopelessly passive sleeper, and even the "teacher's pet" are all struggling in their own ways to gain status, acceptance, and social belonging.

Some students believe that excelling in school work, being first in line, or being first finished with an assignment will gain them the recognition and approval they so desperately seek. Unfortunately, their behavior does not increase their self-confidence or self-reliance; it only perpetuates their dependence on the approval of others.

As Dreikurs warned, there are few influences in a student's life more powerful than the feeling of being rejected by others. The classroom, under the leadership of the teacher, can either provide support and approval for all of its members or it can become an arena for constant competitiveness that builds a crystallized dichotomy of acceptance and rejection. Satisfying the need for belonging and relatedness provides the security necessary for students to risk exploring and expanding the limits of their identity.

A more recent, research-based view of student *relatedness* is provided by James Connell, Richard Ryan, and Edward Deci from the University of Rochester (Connell & Ryan, 1984; Deci & Ryan, 1985). Like Dreikurs, they perceive the desire for relatedness as a basic psychological need of students. In the context of school, Connell defines relatedness as the degree of emotional security that students feel with themselves and with the significant others involved in their lives as students—specifically parents, teachers, and peers. According to the model of student motivation proposed by Connell, Ryan, and Deci, students will feel better about themselves and will be more intrinsically motivated and engaged in their learning when they feel connected rather than isolated or alienated from their schoolmates, teachers, and parents.

Chapter 4 offers ten recommendations and twenty specific motivational strategies that teachers can use to help all students develop a sense of belonging and relatedness in the classroom.

The Need for Self-Esteem

After extensive testimony and deliberation, the California Task Force to Promote Self-Esteem and Personal Social Responsibility defined *self-esteem* as appreciating one's own worth and importance, having the character to be accountable for oneself, and acting responsibly toward others (Reasoner, 1982). This three-part definition is useful to educators who are looking for methods and strategies to increase student self-esteem and intrinsic motivation to learn. Before examining each component of this definition, it may be useful to distinguish the term *self-esteem* from *self-concept*. A person's self-concept is the picture or perception that the individual holds of his or her strengths, weaknesses, abilities, values, and temperament. Self-esteem, like self-worth or self-value, refers to the judgment of merit or value that an individual places on the various facets of the self. For example, a student might have a self-concept that includes being an uncoordinated athlete, but it is the value he places on athletics that determines how this view of himself will affect his self-esteem.

The first component of the California Task Force's definition of self-esteem concerns recognizing the significance of one's inherent worth and importance as a human being. Students' desire to enhance and to protect their sense of self-esteem cause them to seek experiences that generate feelings of pride and accomplishment and to avoid experiences that cause them to feel valueless.

The second component of the Task Force's definition deals with "having the character to be accountable for oneself." Character is derived from a healthy, positive sense of self-worth and must be nurtured both in the home and in the school. Its foundation comes from a loving family. Yet the reality in current classrooms is that many students come to school without having experienced the love and care needed for them to feel good about who they are. To increase the chances of enhancing positive self-esteem in these students, teachers have little choice but to build classroom environments that nurture human integrity, character, and accountability.

The last part of the Task Force definition, "acting responsibly toward others," suggests that all individuals need to learn to respect the uniqueness of others as they learn to value their own. Valuing the differences among others requires that students have a solid base of self-worth and a willingness to listen to the thoughts and feelings of their peers. The insecurities and self-doubt of many students, however, make this a more difficult task than it appears. It requires that teachers consciously and systematically provide activities that help students experience their uniqueness and worth, learn skills of empathic listening, and assume responsibility for their own behavior.

Important to the process of developing positive self-esteem is establishing a sense of identity. Starting when they are young children, the identity of students evolves from the feedback they receive from others and from their own self-evaluation. Teachers play an important part in this development. By using positive information feedback, they can help students establish an awareness of their unique characteristics while they learn to develop more accurate self-descriptions.

This process of establishing a strong sense of self becomes especially important during adolescence and revolves around one's search for an answer to the question "Who am I?" As students struggle to find out who they are and where they are going, they begin to form a solid and secure sense of personal identity. This process of self-definition is not always easily resolved. Some adolescents fail to honestly confront the question of who they are, choosing instead to conform to the more socially acceptable identity described by the expectations of their parents or peers. (Edgar Friedenburg [1959] poignantly describes this process in his book *The Vanishing Adolescent.*)

Other individuals become overwhelmed by the question of self-identity and leave adolescence with a sense of emptiness and confusion. Although periods of confusion are a natural part of the process of establishing a firm identity, these individuals seem to drift aimlessly through their adolescent years, as if trying to cross an ocean in a rudderless boat with no clue about how to control it.

It is easy for teachers to become impatient with the confusion and inconsistency that are frustrating but necessary by-products of self-definition. Students need encouragement to explore their options, feedback on their strengths and weaknesses, and unconditional acceptance if they are to make successful landfalls in the voyage to selfhood.

Chapter 5 offers ten recommendations and twenty specific motivational strategies that teachers can use to help all students develop and maintain a positive sense of self-esteem in the classroom.

The Need for Involvement and Enjoyment

Psychiatrist William Glasser argues that the need for fun is basic to all human beings. Although the word "fun" has many interpretations, it implies the desire of people to seek activities that provide either physical, social, cognitive, or psychological pleasure.

The need for involvement and enjoyment in learning is often lost when educators are restrained when designing curriculum and lesson plans. With increasing pressures to produce clearly defined outcomes, it's understandable why the emphasis on the products of learning can supersede and occasionally obliterate the process of learning. If teachers, however, truly want to intrinsically motivate students to devote large amounts of effort to learning, then they must design the process of learning with a clear understanding of students' need for involvement and enjoyment; failing to do so often makes learning drudgery and the results superficial.

By definition, intrinsically motivating activities provide individuals with fun or enjoyment, although fun and enjoyment need not be limited to intrinsically motivating activities. Many activities undertaken for external goals can also satisfy similar needs. Many teachers, for example, find considerable enjoyment and fun in their jobs, although it seems likely that few would continue to teach if a paycheck did not accompany the activity. Students' desire for involvement and enjoyment in learning is evident when they are asked to describe the teachers in whose classes they are motivated to work their hardest. They invariably describe teachers who are enthusiastic about their course content and find ways to make the learning activities interesting and enjoyable. Yet, as psychologist Raymond Wlodkowski (1978) suggests, too often the word "enjoyable" has a bad reputation in schools. Apparently many educators believe that learning is supposed to be hard work, and if it's enjoyable, it cannot be serious or significant. This argument, however, is repeatedly contradicted by students' descriptions of classrooms in which they were highly motivated to do their best. It is in these classrooms that students are most willing to spend many hours learning content and meeting course objectives.

When teachers reflect on their own experiences as students, they usually confirm the assertion that stimulating and enjoyable learning need not be frivolous; enjoyment and hard work often go hand in hand. As John Dewey wrote many years ago, "When a child feels that his work is a task, it is only under compulsion that he gives himself to it. At every let up of external pressure his attention, released from constraint, flies to what interests him" (1913, p. 2).

Stimulating student interest is more than just exciting their visual or auditory senses. At the heart of enthusiastic teaching is the ability to select instructional procedures and activities that relate to the child's present experience and needs.

Television exploits the passive receptivity of viewers and uses visual and auditory stimulation and repetition to implant images and build product recognition. As educators, however, we need to continually remind ourselves that significant learning requires that students actively construct a personal meaning of what is being taught through the dynamic and interactive processes of analyzing and dissecting new information, and then integrating one's interpretation of this information into that which is already understood. Significant learning generates involvement, and involvement is a prerequisite to commitment and enjoyment of the learning process. In short, when comprehension and application are the goals, the mind must be actively involved in the construction of meaning.

Chapter 6 offers ten recommendations and twenty specific motivational strategies that teachers can use to help stimulate student involvement and enjoyment in learning.

TARGET STRUCTURES

Each of the following 100 motivational strategies identifies the manipulable structures within the classroom that it is capable of influencing. Developed by Epstein (1989), this framework helps teachers identify the areas within a classroom that can contribute to the development of adaptive motivational goals and intrinsic motivation in students. Using the acronym TARGET to label these six structures, she defines task, authority, reward, grouping, evaluation, and time as the categories that can be manipulated by the teacher to create a classroom environment that supports learning goals and intrinsic motivation.

Task Structure (T)

The task structure within a classroom deals with the organization, composition, and design of the learning activities or tasks that teachers require of students. According to Epstein (1989, p. 93), "It includes the content and sequence of the curriculum, the design of classwork and homework, the level of difficulty of the work, and the materials required to complete assignments." Although the specific objectives and outcomes required of a particular grade or class are usually predetermined, most teachers have considerable flexibility in deciding how to design instructional activities to reach these outcomes. The difficulty level and requirements of assignments, for example, may be identical for all students or may be tailored to fit individual or small-group needs. Teachers may design tasks that emphasize a didactic, linear approach or they may plan tasks to emphasize a discovery or problem-solving structure.

To foster achievement goals in all students, it is incumbent upon teachers to structure tasks that provide challenges to both fast- and slow-learning students. By understanding the skills and prior knowledge of students and by tailoring assignments to these individual differences, teachers can design learning activities that are neither too easy for some nor too difficult for others. Clearly stated performance standards may be required of all students, but it is only by varying the structure of learning tasks that all students can experience success through reasonable effort, thereby ensuring progress toward achieving these outcomes.

Authority Structure (A)

The authority structure within the classroom, according to Epstein, concerns the nature of decision making as it occurs between teachers and students. "In some settings, authority is exercised only by the teacher; in other settings, teachers and students share responsibilities for making choices, giving directions, monitoring work, setting and enforcing rules, establishing and offering rewards, and evaluating student success and teacher quality" (1989, p. 94). The primary authority or control within a classroom clearly rests with the teacher. How the teacher shares this control, however, can influence students' commitment to the learning process.

Reward Structure (R)

The reward structure in a classroom, according to Epstein, concerns the procedures and practices used by teachers to reinforce student achievement. Teachers can be highly selective when distributing rewards, or they can be quite generous in deciding what students, behaviors, and achievements are worthy of reinforcement. However, as previously discussed, when rewards are used to undermine student autonomy, they may extinguish intrinsic motivation and undermine self-determination.

Yet rewards do define the achievements and behaviors that teachers consider important, and when rewards are used to convey information about student competence at these activities, they can enhance students' motivation to learn. Epstein believes that in most schools, only a few students receive the official recognition and reinforcement conveyed by rewards. She suggests that if teachers try to keep in mind a student's *history* of past accomplishments and skills, *plans* or goals for which a student is striving, and *outcomes,* or actual accomplishments, it will be possible to design reward structures that more widely acknowledge the efforts and achievements of all students. Knowing a student's past accomplishments and goals, for example, can help teachers keep a record of students' "personal best" accomplishments and thus reward student improvements more fairly. According to Epstein,

> [O]f the three elements of evaluation—history, plans, and outcomes—only outcomes regulate the reward structure in most subjects in most schools. If the reward structure is ignored, teachers may find that their distributions of grades, honors, and other awards support and boost the energies of some students, while the same practices alienate and destroy the energies of others. (1989, p. 95)

Grouping Structure (G)

The grouping structure concerns the manner in which students are segregated and grouped for instructional activities. Few practices in education are as controversial as grouping and tracking students according to their academic ability. Those who argue in favor of ability grouping believe that teachers can do a better job of meeting student needs when the variance in student achievement is reduced through combining or tracking students of similar abilities. The strongest support for ability grouping seems to come from those concerned with the effects of heterogeneous groups on the more able students. Clearly, it is beyond the scope of this discussion to explore the arguments and research supporting and refuting each position on ability grouping. As Oakes (1988, p. 42) suggests, however, as "educators become increasingly disenchanted with tracking, they may not need to throw out the baby (possible benefits to the top students) with the bath water (likely disadvantages to the rest)." By viewing ability as a malleable rather than fixed trait and by restructuring classrooms to allow for differences in learning speeds, it may be possible for students of all abilities to benefit from being taught together. Ames (1990) suggests that when classrooms provide flexible and heterogeneous grouping arrangements, and when they allow students multiple grouping opportunities, the intrinsic motivation of students in the classroom can be enhanced.

Evaluation Structure (E)

The fifth classroom structure identified by the TARGET acronym that supports mastery goals and intrinsic motivation is evaluation. This structure concerns the manner by which teachers establish expectations and measure and judge student performance relative to these expectations. Raffini (1993) provides an extended discussion of the effects of criterion and norm-referenced evaluation procedures on student motivation to learn. That discussion will not be repeated here. The following comments by Epstein should suffice:

> *An effective evaluation structure—with important, challenging, yet attainable standards, fair and clear procedures for monitoring progress, and explicit and frequent information about progress—should lead students to a higher level of understanding about their own effort, abilities and improvement. An ineffective structure can embarrass or confuse students and misdirect their efforts for improvement, by withholding information on what and how to improve, or by setting standards too high to attain (1989, p. 97)*

Since norm-referenced evaluation artificially restricts the number of students that can experience success, it seems evident that when student achievement is compared to clearly stated performance standards and when students are given adequate time to master necessary skills, most students will be motivated to learn, since they will have a reasonable opportunity to experience success from their efforts.

Time Structure (T)

The final manipulable classroom structure that can foster mastery goals and support intrinsic motivation in students is the amount of time allocated to learning tasks. Spady (1988) argues that the current educational paradigm is based on keeping instructional time a constant. Biology, for example, is usually what high school students learn for 45 minutes a day during the 180 instructional days of their freshman or sophomore year. Of course, achievement in biology varies considerably among students. Spady argues that outcome-based learning is designed around a major reversal in these variables; achievement needs to become the constant, and time the variable. If we want all students to attain the same high level of mastery or competence in biology, then we may need to allow slower-learning students 45, 60, or 90 minutes a day for 180, 250, or even 300 instructional days. If a high level of achievement is to be a constant, then time *must* be a variable.

CHAPTER TWO

Strategies for Enhancing Student Autonomy

Students' need for a sense of autonomy or self-determination significantly influences their intrinsic motivation to learn in the classroom. Whatever their grade level, students want the freedom to decide for themselves what activities to undertake and what behaviors to adopt. This need to control the decisions that affect one's life lies at the foundation of intrinsic motivation. The need for self-determination is satisfied when both teachers and students are free to act of their own volition, rather than repeatedly being coerced to behave according to the wishes of some higher authority.

The single most important strategy for building a sense of autonomy in students is to provide them with *choices*. It is learning to make choices that leads to commitment, and it is commitment that leads to responsibility. In turn, it is responsibility, or the willingness to be held accountable for one's decisions, that leads to feelings of self-determination and autonomy.

RECOMMENDATIONS FOR ENHANCING STUDENT AUTONOMY

1. *When several learning activities meet the same objective, allow students to choose among them.* Although this suggestion may make the teacher's job more difficult, it is a powerful method for building student self-determination and intrinsic motivation to learn.

2. *When classroom procedures are not critical, allow students options in deciding how to implement them.* Any choice, whatever size, contributes to student autonomy.

3. *Whenever possible, provide opportunities for students to decide when, where, and in what order to complete assignments.* When faced with choices and decisions, students are required to make a commitment; it is this commitment that leads to autonomous, intrinsically motivated behavior.

4. *Create a psychologically safe environment in which students are willing to risk making choices.* Feelings of insecurity and lack of self-confidence make it difficult for some students to choose from alternatives. Protecting students from the ridicule and criticism of others and reminding them that mistakes are a necessary and natural part of the learning process can help to create a psychologically safe classroom.

5. *When student behavior must be restricted or limited, take time to provide clear and logical explanations of the reasoning behind the limits.* "Because I said so!" is simply not good enough.

6. *When behavior must be restricted, acknowledge conflicting feelings.* Acknowledging conflicting feelings lets students know that their thoughts and emotions are being understood.

7. *When behavior must be required or restricted, use minimumly sufficient controls.* When external controls are necessary, using the least control possible can help teachers meet their objective while increasing the likelihood that students will eventually internalize the necessity for the restriction or requirement.

8. *Use logical consequences rather than punishment when a student's behavior makes it difficult to teach others.* Since logical consequences emphasize the reality of the social order, rather than the personal power of the teacher, they are more likely to enhance a sense of autonomy by helping students assume ownership for their behavior; punishment places this responsibility with the teacher.

9. *Whenever possible, encourage students to use the skills of individual goal-setting to define, monitor, and achieve self-determined objectives.* Helping students verbalize and affirm realistic goals increases intrinsic motivation by putting students in control of their aspirations and behaviors.

10. *Try to avoid making students right, wrong, good, or bad for their actions. Rather, hold them accountable for the consequences of their choices.* Students learn to evaluate alternatives when they are held accountable for the consequences of their choices, rather than judged or labeled.

Round Tuits

Purpose

The purpose of this strategy is to enable students to experience a sense of autonomy and control regarding homework assignments.

TARGET Areas

Authority; Time

Grade Level

This strategy can be adapted to all grade levels and content areas in which homework is assigned and evaluated.

Procedure

This strategy allows students one or two opportunities per grading period to forgo an assignment without penalty. At the beginning of each grading period, all students are given one or two round tuits (see Figure 2.1) to use any time that they do not get "around to" doing a homework assignment. No excuses or explanations are necessary when the student hands in his or her round tuit for the homework assignment. All students, of course, are still expected to master the material assigned.

FIGURE 2.1 Round Tuits

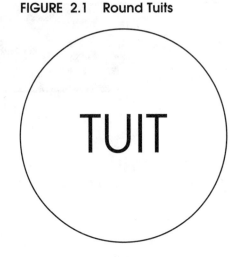

To prevent a black market of round tuits, the teacher should make it clear that students get only two tuits per grading period. Teachers can record their use in their grade books. Teachers will discover that some students will use their round tuits early in the semester while others will save them. Those who do not use their tuits can be given the option of turning them back for free time or using them for bonus points to be added to their grade average.

Teachers can make round tuits from laminated paper, cardboard, or thin plywood. They are also available from Sillcocks Plastics International, Inc., 310 Snyder Ave., Berkeley Heights, NJ 07922, 1–800–526–4919.

Variations

In addition to homework, teachers can use round tuits for other requirements, or for trips to the lavatory or drinking fountain.

2.2

Newsroom

Purpose

This strategy builds a sense of autonomy by allowing students to choose information that they will include in the class's weekly newsletter. Group relatedness is also developed as students share the personal information in their entries.

TARGET Areas

Task; Authority; Recognition; Grouping; Evaluation

Grade Level

This strategy can be adapted to almost all elementary grade levels.

Procedure

Students are encouraged to contribute to a weekly classroom newsletter that will be duplicated and sent home. Students are asked to write about only those activities that take place in school.

To help students get started, the teacher writes the headings *Yesterday* and *News in the Making* on the chalkboard. Students are then asked to write a sentence under either topic that relates to something that happened in school. Since the goal is to help the class become better writers, the group can offer editing suggestions to each author. Although authors are required to correct obvious grammatical mistakes, they can choose what style changes to make. When the sentences are completed, the authors transfer their sentences to a newsletter sheet that is duplicated on Friday and sent home with each child.

Variations

Space and time constraints may make it necessary for the teacher to limit the number of sentences written each week. The writers could be selected on a rotating basis and a rotating editorial team could be used to suggest corrections. Other volunteers could be used to enter the sentences into the class computer to simplify editing and printing. Schools with access to more advanced technology could scan in examples of student art work to be included with the newsletter. Depending on the grade level, some students might want to write short-paragraph descriptions of classroom activities.

Source: Gina Bailey, second grade.

Goal Cards

Purpose

This strategy can help all students experience autonomy and success by encouraging them to select and achieve individually determined goals. These goals represent clearly stated criteria that each student can use to define his or her personal standard of success.

TARGET Areas

Task; Authority; Recognition; Evaluation; Time

Grade Level

This strategy is useful in upper elementary, middle, and high school grades in all content areas.

Procedure

Students are told that they are going to construct their personal goal cards. Like credit cards, they should be kept in a secure and protected place; because they are personal, students should be encouraged not to share them with anyone. Next, ask students to reflect on the various goals they hope to achieve in the future. These might include things like going to college, getting a car, finding a good job, or simply getting a passing grade on next week's math test. Students are then given three by five index cards and asked to write the phrase "Short-Term Goals" on the top center of one side of the card and the phrase "Long-Term Goals" on the top center of the other side (see Figure 2.2). The teacher then instructs the students to draw a line below the headings to separate the card into two halves. They should do this on both sides of the card. (Teachers may want to draw Figure 2.2 on the chalkboard as they explain these directions.) Starting with the "Long-Term Goals," students are asked to think of two personal or career goals that they hope to accomplish after they finish high school. They may want to list several goals on a piece of scratch paper before they select the two most important. When they have com-

FIGURE 2.2 Goal Cards

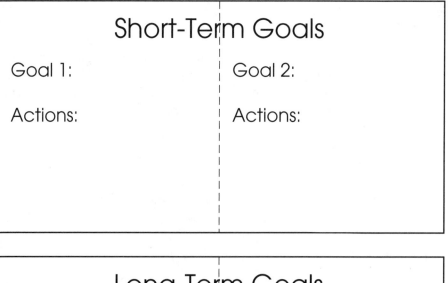

pleted this task, ask students to write the first goal on one side of the line and the second goal on the other side.

Next, have the students turn the card to the "Short-Term Goal" side and think of two important goals that they hope to accomplish within the next month. These should be written on either side of the dividing line.

Staying with the short-term goals, students are now asked to think of three to five specific things that they can do to help them achieve each goal. For example, if a student's goal is to get an A on an English paper, then he or she may decide to:

- Spend at least two hours per day working on the paper
- Use note cards to help organize and keep track of ideas
- Outline the paper before starting to write
- Have a friend proofread the first copy of the paper
- Reread the sections in the textbook that deal with writing papers

After students have had enough time to write down their ideas on how they are going to achieve their two short-term goals, they should be encouraged to estimate the probability of achieving each goal. Next, have the students turn the card over and write down specific things that they can do to help them achieve their long-term goals. For example, if a student's goal is to become an electronics technician, then he or she might decide to:

- Stop in the guidance office or library to find information about the training needed to become an electronic technician
- Call three vocational and technical schools to find out what types of programs they have in electronics
- Interview an electronics technician to find out how he or she likes the job
- Maintain an A or B average in electronics class
- Spend a day visiting a technical school that has a program in electronics

After students have finished constructing their goal cards, they should be encouraged to keep them in a safe place and to review them frequently to keep track of their progress. The teacher can conduct occasional class discussions that focus on students' progress toward reaching their goals and any difficulties they may be having carrying out their goal actions. Students can also reflect on their accuracy in estimating the probability of reaching their short-term goals. This could lead to a discussion of the differences between realistic and unrealistic goals and how these relate to feelings of success.

Variations

The teacher might want to give students practice in setting and reaching weekly and monthly goals before focusing on long-term goals. Students might also discuss how they can reward themselves when they reach their goals.

Floating A

Purpose

This strategy is designed to foster student autonomy and self-determination in regard to evaluation and grades. By selecting how and when to use a Floating A coupon, students feel a sense of self-determination and control over the grading system.

TARGET Areas

Authority; Evaluation

Grade Level

This strategy is useful in any classroom where grades are used to evaluate student performance.

Procedure

Design a Floating A coupon similar to that shown in Figure 2.3. Duplicate enough to give each student one coupon per subject for each grading period. Students are informed that they can use the coupon to exchange their grade on any assignment (you may want to exclude unit tests) for a grade of A. Students have up to twenty-four hours after receiving an assignment grade to use the Floating A coupon. Students who do not use

FIGURE 2.3   Floating A

Floating A

This coupon can be used
to exchange
one homework grade
for an A

Subject: _____

Name: _____

the coupon by the end of the grading period can simply add the Floating A to be averaged with all previous grades. By instructing students to write their names on the coupons when they are distributed, the teacher can avoid a "black market" economy for Floating A coupons.

Variations

The teacher may choose to allow students to transfer Floating A coupons to subsequent grading periods.

Source: Adapted by Barbara Isaacson, elementary school principal.

Quality Checklist

Purpose

This strategy is designed to help all students experience feelings of autonomy and competence. By learning to identify the characteristics of quality essays, students can gain control over the evaluation and quality of their own writing.

TARGET Areas

Task; Authority; Evaluation; Time

Grade Level

This strategy is particularly useful in middle and high school English classes, but it can be easily adapted to almost all grade levels and content areas.

Procedure

Using small groups, ask students to brainstorm the qualities that make writing exciting to read. Using their lists, lead a discussion on what makes a piece of writing average, good, or excellent, recording their comments on the chalkboard or on an overhead transparency. Also discuss any difficulties they may have evaluating the quality of their own writing.

Next, have students examine the last essay they wrote to determine those areas that could benefit from more effort. Allow students time to practice evaluating their work on this simple dimension. They might, for example, simply identify at the end of their next writing assignment the best part of the essay and the part that could benefit from more development. Meanwhile, using the results of the earlier brainstorm on exciting writing and the discussion on average, good, and excellent writing, develop a checklist similar to the one that follows:

A Quality Theme Has:

_____Neat penmanship

_____Interesting sentences

_____Exciting and descriptive words

_____Combined sentences rather than short, choppy ones

_____Correct spelling

_____Paragraphs that contain one major idea

_____Correct punctuation

Duplicate copies of the enclosed checklist and ask students to use it while they are writing their next theme and attach it when the theme is finished. To give students practice in using the checklist, have them work in small groups and use the checklist to evaluate several themes from previous years (names omitted). The groups can compare their results and discuss any differences. Finally, the teacher may find it helpful to use the checklist when evaluating student themes, giving scores or ratings on each item. Differences between the students' and the teacher's rating can be discussed.

Variations

Checklists can be developed for assignments in areas other than English. If the teacher assigns letter or number grades to written assignments in science or history, for example, students could improve their skill at self-evaluation if they were given an opportunity to make similar judgments. This could be easily accomplished by using a quality checklist with blanks for both teacher and student evaluations.

Source: Adapted from Tom Baumgart, middle school teacher.

2.6

Pick Your Points

Purpose

This strategy builds autonomy and self-determination by allowing students to have a choice in the selection of supplementary reading.

TARGET Areas

Task; Authority; Evaluation; Time

Grade Level

This strategy can be used in almost any content area in upper elementary, middle, and high school.

Procedure

Before carrying out this strategy the teacher should collect a large variety of articles on a particular topic that the class will be studying. The articles can be from books on the subject, teacher's guides, periodicals, or children's literature. The goal is to collect as many resources as possible that reflect a full spectrum of reading levels. On a topic such as rainforests, for example, hundreds of articles can be found that require elementary to college reading levels.

After obtaining a large collection of material, the teacher rates each article or excerpt on a scale of one to five according to reading level, length, and complexity. The number is then placed in an upper corner of the selection.

Based on the length of the unit, students can be required to accumulate a predetermined number of supplementary reading points for each grade level. For example, to earn a grade of C on a particular unit, students must accumulate at least five supplementary reading points; to earn a B, seven points are required; and an A requires ten points.

When students have finished their reading, they can be asked to complete a reading report that could include the following questions:

1. In two or three sentences, please summarize the main idea of the article.
2. List at least three facts that you learned from your article that others might find interesting.
3. What was the most important thing that you learned from the article? Why?
4. Discuss something from the article with which you either agreed or disagreed.
5. From the information in the article, what predictions could you make about the future?

Based on the answers to these questions, the teacher may award the points specified or may ask students to make revisions or additions.

Variations

Students could be asked to help build the reading collection by seeking out articles on their own. In collaboration with the teacher, point values could be assigned after the student has read the article. Three-ring binders could be used to store articles of various point values. Collections of these binders could then be used as resources for topics discussed in the class. Articles could also be stapled into manila folders and kept in a file cabinet.

Source: Harold Beedle, middle school social studies teacher.

Check It Out

Purpose

This strategy provides students with a sense of autonomy by allowing them to choose one or more skill areas they would like to have evaluated during a specific assignment. This strategy also supports students' competence by enabling them to concentrate on specific skills they want to improve.

TARGET Areas

Authority; Evaluation

Grade Level

This strategy can be adapted to almost all grade levels where basic writing skills are emphasized.

Procedure

After the teacher has provided instruction in various writing skills such as using complete sentences, proper capitalization, appropriate punctuation, or creativity, written work is evaluated according to the "Check It Out" procedure. When students turn in their written assignments, they use a rubber stamp or similar procedure to identify the skill areas that they want the teacher to evaluate or "check out." Figure 2.4 provides several examples of the types of stamps that might be made for this purpose.

After stamping their papers, students check the box or boxes that identify the skills that they would like the teacher to evaluate. When reading the papers, the teacher focuses only on the skills checked by the student. This allows papers to be returned with fewer errors. Since students eventually will be required to master the full spectrum of writing skills, they may choose to have several areas evaluated on any given paper.

Variations

Depending on the grade level of students, many variations in this strategy are possible. It can be adapted to the teacher's personal grading system and objectives by identifying specific writing skills and developing appropriate stamps. The teacher can also prescribe progressions to two, three, or four skills, depending on skills of the students. The punctuation category could also be subdivided into commas, periods, quotation marks, etc.

Source: Kimberly Kirk, first grade teacher.

FIGURE 2.4 Check It Out Stamps

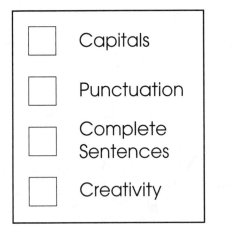
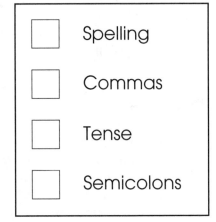

Self-Awareness
and Career Choice

Purpose

Personal preferences play an important role in career choice. This strategy is designed to support student autonomy and self-awareness within the context of career choice.

TARGET Areas

Task; Authority; Grouping

Grade Level

This strategy is most appropriate for middle and high school students.

Procedure

Read the following scenario to your students.

> *Imagine that you have applied for a summer job at a local corporation. The personnel director informs you that they have six divisions within the company and that you must decide in which division you would like to*

35

work. All divisions pay the same for summer work and once you select a division, you cannot switch to another. You are also told that there is a good possibility that you could have a permanent career within the division that you select.

The Six Corporate Divisions are:

Production—In this division you will be doing clearly defined jobs that are directly involved in product manufacturing such as handling materials, tools, or machines. You will be working with others at tasks that are systematic and organized.

Processing—In this division you will process orders, keep records, file materials, and correspond with suppliers and customers. You will use computer spreadsheets for billing and accounting, duplicating and fax machines for correspondence, and word processors for other tasks.

Management—In this division you will manage others. You will try to help employees behave responsibly and do their jobs more efficiently. You will also be responsible for helping corporate stockholders realize a profit from their investment.

Research—In this division you will investigate and gather data to improve production effectiveness, analyze new technologies, and observe consumer interest in new product lines. You will also conduct a survey and analyze its data to increase sales markets.

Advertising—In this division you will use your artistic and creative abilities to help develop new advertising campaigns and product packaging. You will have a great deal of unstructured time to develop your own ideas that will eventually be evaluated in consumer test markets.

Personnel—In this division you will be responsible for working with employees individually and in small groups to train them in new job skills. You will also help employees deal with their personal problems and take full advantage of their job benefits.

Ask students to write on a slip of paper the division in which they would *most* like to work. Ask them to skip four spaces and write the division in which they would *least* like to work. Next, ask them to rank the other four divisions from most liked to least liked and place these divisions on the four blanks between the most and least liked. When each student has ranked the divisions, ask them to walk around the room sharing their lists to see if they can find students with the same ranking as their own.

Using the six divisions of the company, ask students to form groups based on the division they prefer the most. When the groups are formed, ask each group to list as many jobs as they can that have characteristics similar to those in their division. These lists can be shared with the class.

Depending on the time available, corporate groups can be formed with one person from each of the six divisions. They might discuss why they made their choices and how their choices would complement their personal needs while meeting corporate goals.

Variations

Duplicate the job descriptions or write them on the chalkboard or an overhead. Students could use the library to research a particular job that would fall within their division. They also could be asked to interview someone who works in a job similar to the type in which they are interested.

Goal Books

Purpose

This strategy can foster autonomy and self-determination by helping students keep a record of their academic goals and monitor their progress toward reaching them.

TARGET Areas

Task; Authority; Time

Grade Level

This strategy can be adapted to almost all grade levels and content areas.

Procedure

All students should be encouraged to purchase a separate notebook or set aside a section of their assignment notebook to record specific goals that they establish for each of their subjects. Middle and high school teachers can encourage students to set goals on a unit or monthly basis, or according to grading periods. As in the example below, students can organize their goals in an outline form with Roman numerals representing subjects or units, capital letters representing individual goals, and numbers representing specific details or steps to achieving each goal.

GOAL OUTLINE EXAMPLE

Month: October

  I. History
      A. Learn the reasons that the Pilgrims came to America
          1. Review the three reasons identified on page 128 of the text
      B. Complete reading assignments on time
      C. Pay attention and take notes during films
  II. Math
      A. Get at least 90% correct on the fractions test
          1. Memorize the rules for adding and subtracting fractions
          2. Do all practice problems
 III. Language Arts
      A. Read one library book each week
          1. Spend at least thirty minutes per day, including weekends, reading library books
      B. Complete all writing assignments and hand them in on time

Some teachers find it useful to take fifteen or twenty minutes every Monday for students to update their goal books. Students can check off goals achieved, and they can formulate new goals for the unit or month ahead.

Variations

When computers are available, teachers can encourage students to keep their goals on a floppy goal disk or in a locked folder on the hard drive. The process of updating and monitoring goals can then become both personally and technologically rewarding.

Teachers can periodically schedule short goal conferences with students to discuss their goals and to review each student's progress in reaching them. Students can also share their goals in small groups and then work together to reach their goals.

Source: Tammi Torrence, special education teacher.

Kid Questions

Purpose

This strategy can enhance feelings of autonomy and self-determination by allowing students to assist in writing questions for evaluating content mastery. It also can increase students' feelings of competence by providing a content and skill review, and by providing practice in selecting the most important content from reading assignments.

TARGET Areas

Task; Authority; Grouping; Evaluation

Grade Level

This strategy can be adapted to almost all grade levels and content areas in which formative or summative test questions are administered.

Procedure

Teachers can use this strategy with individuals or with small groups. Before beginning the activity, it will be helpful for the teacher to discuss the following two major distinctions between the types of questions usually asked on a test:

A. Memorization questions—These are questions that measure students' ability to recall important factual information.

Examples:

- Who was the first president of the United States?
- What is the formula for the area of a circle?

B. Interpretation questions—These questions ask students to interpret meaning from information or to use information to solve problems.

Examples:

- Explain how a candidate for president of the United States might win a majority of the votes cast, but still lose the election.
- What is the area of a circle with a six-inch diameter?

If students will be tested over a certain amount of reading material, group the students and divide the reading material among the groups. Based on the number of pages and the grade level of the students, explain that each group will be responsible for writing a certain number of memorization questions and a certain number of interpretation questions from their section of the reading assignment. Ask the groups to ensure that each group member contribute at least one question.

At the completion of the task, assemble the questions into a test on the material assigned. Explain to the class that the teacher reserves the right to add or to edit questions to meet the content objectives for the unit.

When possible, teachers should encourage students to write interpretation questions that are relevant to their lives. For example, in a unit on percentages, a group could write a word problem that asks students to calculate the percentage of total yards gained by a certain player in a recent football game.

Variations

Kid questions can be used for review purposes or as part of a chapter or unit exam. The questions can also be used as an individual homework assignment rather than as a group project.

Source: Sally Yakel, math and study skills teacher.

2.11

Sentence Polishing

Purpose

The strategy builds autonomy and self-determination by helping students realize that there are many ways to combine words to express an idea.

TARGET Areas

Task; Authority; Recognition; Grouping; Evaluation; Time

Grade Level

This strategy is useful for upper elementary, middle, and high school language arts and English classes.

Procedure

The teacher starts this lesson by explaining to the class that there are many different ways to say the same thing. The teacher could demonstrate this by writing the following sentences on the chalkboard or on an overhead:

My father is a pilot, so he's not home very often.

My dad is not home much because he's a pilot.

My dad, a pilot, is always away from home.

My pop is not around too much because he's a pilot.

My father is a commercial aviator; therefore, he is frequently away from home.

My dad is always gone; he's a pilot.

My pa flies planes so he's not home very much.

Because my father is a pilot, he doesn't spend much time at home.

The teacher asks students to work with a partner to see how many variations they can produce from a sentence they make up or from one provided by the teacher. After the students share some of their examples, the teacher emphasizes how rewording or rearranging the words in a sentence can often make it communicate more clearly. Students are then asked to identify which sentences from a set of examples sound the best and communicate more clearly. Students will usually have several opinions regarding which sentences they think are best. These differences allow the teacher to emphasize that writers have to make their own decisions regarding how they want their writing to sound. The teacher can help the class realize that this decision is often based on the audience to which the writer is communicating.

Variations

The teacher could compile several sets of examples and ask students to pick out the sentences that they think sound awkward and those that seem to communicate clearly. They could then help the teacher reword the sentences to communicate more effectively. Depending on the grade level, the teacher can expand on this experience with a discussion of writing style, word order, content, or mood.

Source: Bill Andersen, middle school language arts teacher.

Self-Report Card

Purpose

This strategy provides students with a sense of autonomy by providing them with an opportunity to evaluate their own performance.

TARGET Areas

Task; Authority; Evaluation

Grade Level

This strategy can be adapted to upper elementary, middle, and high school.

Procedure

This strategy requires that teachers develop a self-report form that students can use to evaluate their progress in the same content areas being evaluated by the teacher on the school's report card. Figure 2.5 provides an example of a self-report card that can be used in elementary classrooms. A form with similar questions could be developed for middle and high school classes.

After students have had time to complete the self-report card, teachers should collect the cards and compare the students' evaluations with their own. It is particularly important to identify any discrepancies between the two evaluations and to discuss these discrepancies with the student.

FIGURE 2.5   Self-Report Card

Name _____

Reading

1. Approximately how many pages of outside reading have you completed this
   quarter?_____

2. In what ways can you improve your efforts in reading? _____

3. Have you kept up with your daily assignments in your workbook and
   reading text? _____

4. How can you improve the quality of your work in reading? _____

5. What grade do you deserve in reading? _____

Skills_____ Effort _____

Math

1. Have you worked hard to get all of your assignments completed on time? _____

2. Are there any math skills from this quarter that you are still unsure of? _____

   If so, which ones? _____

3. What ways can you improve your efforts in math? _____

4. What grade do you deserve in math? _____

Skills_____ Effort _____

Spelling

1. Have you been studying your word list each week? _____

2. Do you think you remember the words that you learn to spell each week? _____

3. How do you think you can improve your skill at spelling? _____

4. How well do you spell your words in your creative writing and daily assignments?
   (Circle one)

Superior   very good   fair   not very well

5. What grade should you receive in spelling this quarter? _____

Skills_____ Effort _____

Cursive Writing

1. What grade do you think you have earned this quarter in cursive writing? _____

Skills_____ Effort _____

2. What do you need to work on? _____

Continued

FIGURE 2.5 *Continued*

Science, Social Studies, Art, Music

1. What grade would you give yourself in each of these areas this quarter?

Science: Skills _____ Effort _____

Reason: _____

Social Studies: Skills _____ Effort _____

Reason: _____

Art: Skills _____ Effort _____

Reason: _____

Music: Skills _____ Effort _____

Reason: _____

2. In which areas are you doing at school? _____

3. What do you need to work on? _____

4. In what ways do you think you have improved this quarter? _____

Adapted with permission from: Jones, V., & Jones, L. (1990). *Comprehensive classroom management* (3rd ed.). Boston: Allyn and Bacon, Inc.

Students are often amazingly accurate in their self-evaluations and they can provide teachers with valuable insights into their reasoning about the grades they believe they should receive. If the students have been involved in goal-setting, they can also be asked to write a short statement about the degree of success they have had in reaching their goals. The self-report cards are especially useful to share with parents during teacher-parent conferences. (If the teacher decides to use them for this purpose, it is important to inform students of this decision.) Students seem to enjoy having input into the grades that they receive and appreciate having their opinions considered.

Variations

Teachers may decide to use the self-report cards only at the beginning of the year when they have little knowledge about students' study habits or attitudes toward school. Younger students can participate in the procedure if they are given assistance in completing the form, or if the form is modified to their level.

Source: Jeanne Koblewski, sixth grade elementary school teacher; Jones & Jones (1990).

2.13

Social Studies Hot Seat

Purpose

This strategy enables all students to experience feelings of autonomy and self-determination. It also helps them develop a sense of competence and belonging.

TARGET Areas

Task; Authority; Recognition; Grouping; Evaluation

Grade Level

This strategy is appropriate to almost all grade levels that have mastery of social studies as a main objective.

Procedure

Each student is given a reading assignment from their text, the local newspaper, or from a weekly reader. After they have completed the reading assignment, the teacher assigns the students to cooperative groups and asks each group to construct from seven to ten questions about the reading material. (It is important to the second part of this activity to establish an even number of groups.) Before the groups start on the task, the teacher explains how some questions measure only factual material, others measure comprehension of major ideas or relationships, and still others measure problem-solving skills using inference or statistical computation. Next, the teacher asks each group to write approximately three questions, with answers, for each of these three categories. Depending on the age of the group, it may be useful to present examples to ensure that all students understand the differences among the three categories. When the students finish, the teacher collects the questions, keeping them separated by groups.

Next, the teacher combines the groups into two teams (this part of the activity can be done immediately or on a different day). Two chairs are set in the front of the classroom (one for each team) and are designated "hot seats." The teacher asks for a volunteer from each team to serve as the scorers.

During each round, the teacher asks one member from each team to sit in the hot seat and to choose a factual question for one point, a comprehension question for two points, or a problem-solving question for three points. The teacher then selects a question from the appropriate category from the opposite team's questions. If possible, the teacher might try to match the difficulty level of the question to the skill level of the student. The teacher determines if a question is answered correctly and the scorers mark the results on the chalkboard. A round finishes when each team member has had a chance in the hot seat. Depending on the number of questions, two or three rounds can usually be completed.

Students in Mrs. Prahl's third-grade class at Kegonsa Elementary School, Stoughton, WI participate in a Social Studies Hot Seat discussion

As students review their team's score and make decisions regarding the type of question to choose, their sense of autonomy is enhanced.

Variations

Students may have difficulty constructing questions in the comprehension and problem-solving categories. The teacher can help by adding a number of these questions to the team lists. This activity can also be adapted to content from other areas of the curriculum.

Source: Patricia Prahl, third grade teacher.

Advanced Organizer

Purpose

This strategy supports autonomy and self-determination by providing students with an opportunity to choose the focus of a topic of study.

TARGET Areas

Task; Authority

Grade Level

This strategy can be adapted to almost all grade levels and content areas.

Procedure

A few weeks before starting a new topic or course of study, introduce the subject to the students by mentioning that they will be studying the topic in a few weeks. For example, if you are going to be studying Japan in your social studies curriculum, let the students know this two or three weeks ahead. When you introduce the upcoming unit, encourage students to make a list of the questions they may have and the specific information they would like to learn about Japan. Several days after mentioning the topic, conduct a discussion of student questions and interests and what they would like to learn about Japan.

Using the questions provided by the students, organize your study of the topic around these student interests. For example, students may be interested in Japanese schools, foods, and recreation. Your goal will be to incorporate these interests with the curriculum. Conducting the discussion of student questions and interests two or three weeks before you begin the unit will give you time to pull together a variety of resources as you plan the unit around your students' questions.

Variations

The results of the advanced organizer can be used to assign topics for cooperative learning activities when you begin the unit. Students can also be encouraged to follow their interests through independent research and then present their findings to the class. Librarians and media specialists can be a valuable resource for finding materials relating to student interests. Guest speakers can also be used as a resource for addressing student questions.

Source: Mary Stodola, elementary school teacher.

Peacemakers

Purpose

This strategy enables students to experience a sense of control and autonomy over conflicts that arise on the playground.

TARGET Areas

Task; Authority; Recognition

Grade Level

This strategy is most appropriate for intermediate grades.

Procedure

Depending on the size of the school, three or four students from each intermediate classroom are selected to become members of the "Peacemakers," a group of students who are trained to help solve common recess problems. Several methods of selection are possible: Students can elect representatives, the teacher can appoint representatives, or students can be randomly selected from a group of volunteers. It is important to avoid undermining student autonomy by using membership in the Peacemakers as a bribe or incentive for desired behavior (see Deci & Ryan, 1985; Kohn, 1993; or Raffini, 1993).

This strategy requires that a teacher, counselor, or member of the school administration assume responsibility to serve as the advisor for the Peacemakers, arrange or conduct group training in conflict resolution skills for the group, and be willing to hold weekly or monthly meetings to discuss difficulties they may have in performing their role.

The following books may be useful in organizing and conducting conflict resolution training for the group:

BERMAN, S., & LaFARGE, P. (1993). *Promising practices in teaching social responsibility*. Albany: State University of New York Press.

SCHMIDT, F. (1993). *Peacemaking skills for little kids* (2nd ed.). Peace Works Series. Miami Beach: Peace Education Foundation.

SCHRUMPF, F., CRAWFORD, D., & USADEL, C. (1991). *Peer mediation: Conflict resolution in schools*. Champaign, IL: Research Press.

Advisors may find it helpful to make a stack of 3×5 cards with an example of a playground problem situation written on each card. The cards can then be used to select problems for members of the Peacemakers to role play. By emphasizing fairness, consistency, and good listening skills, the Peacemakers can establish a positive reputation for being helpful.

After training, each member is assigned approximately one playground duty per week. Again, depending on the size of the school, two to four Peacemakers should be on duty at each recess or lunch break. For each problem situation encountered, a Peacemaker writes down a description of the problem, who was involved, and how the problem was solved. These slips are given to the Peacemakers' advisor or to the playground supervisor. It is useful to keep the slips for future training and role playing. It is important that members of Peacemakers see their role as assisting in finding mutually agreed-on solutions rather than as judgment makers or dispensers of punishment. It is also important that a playground supervisor always be available as a referral source for the Peacemakers.

Variations

Peacemakers jackets made or purchased by the PTO can help build a sense of cohesion and identity for members. Some schools may want to rotate membership to provide an opportunity for all students to become members of the Peacemakers. In these situations, class time could be used to train students in conflict resolution skills and for role playing problem situations.

Source: Adapted from Lori Pfeiffer, elementary school teacher.

2.16

Wellness Awareness

Purpose

This strategy enhances student autonomy and enables all students to experience success and competence.

TARGET Areas

Task; Authority; Evaluation

Grade Level

This strategy is most appropriate for middle and high school health classes.

Procedure

After discussing the issue of wellness and how it relates to nutrition, physical fitness, stress management, health, safety, and self-image, invite students to establish their own six-week wellness program. (Filmstrips and videos on health and wellness will be useful to introduce students to the importance of this area of study, and for emphasizing how people's lifestyle choices are directly related to their wellness.) Distribute two copies of the form in Figure 2.6, or your own version, to each student. Tell them that they are to complete both copies, one to be collected today

FIGURE 2.6 Wellness Program

Name _____ Starting Date _____

Date Due _____ Ending Date _____

Please complete both copies of this handout. Keep one in your journal and give the other to your teacher in two days.

Circle the **primary goal** area for your program:

Nutrition   Physical Fitness   Stress Management   Health & Safety   Self-Image

Long-Range Goal: _____

Short-Term Goals (Two weeks):

1. _____ Dates: _____

2. _____ Dates: _____

3. _____ Dates: _____

Reward (Should be received after each short-term goal is achieved):

Reward for goal 1 _____

Reward for goal 2 _____

Reward for goal 3 _____

Program Support:

Who will help you stay on this program? _____

What will they do for or with you? _____

Directions:

Please design your wellness program around your own needs. Set your long-term goal in an area in which you know you can experience some success. Set a reasonable long-term goal that can be attained in about six weeks. Each of the short-term goals should be attainable every two weeks. Please try to set specific and measurable goals (e.g., instead of "lose 6 to 8 pounds," use "7 pounds.").

Please record the results of your program in a daily journal, making an entry each day during the six weeks of your program. Record any information that relates to your goal. Write what you did or didn't do for that day. If you had a day in which you did nothing toward meeting your goal, write that down also.

Every Sunday of your program, use a separate sheet of paper to prepare a weekly summary. This should include information about your weekly progress toward your short- and long-term goals, whether you are enjoying the program or disliking it, the amount of support you are receiving from others, and any other information you would like to share. Please hand in your Sunday summaries at the end of the second, fourth, and final weeks of the program.

Continued

FIGURE 2.6 *Continued*

Evaluation:

At the completion of the six weeks of your program, submit a summary of the entire program. Discuss items like: your total progress during the six weeks, the reasons you were successful or unsuccessful in reaching your long-range goal, whether you plan to continue the program, the reaction of others toward your program, and how you felt physically and mentally during your program. Please provide an honest discussion of the program and the amount of effort you put toward reaching your goals.

and the second to hand in with their personal log at the completion of the six-week program.

Explain to the students that they will have an opportunity to establish their own six-week, long-term wellness goal dealing with any of the five components of wellness: nutrition, physical fitness, stress management, health and safety, and self-image. They will also be asked to establish two short-term goals that can be reached in two-week periods. Long-term wellness goals might include things like weight loss, healthy eating, stress reduction exercises, improving physical fitness, changing thoughts and opinions, or changing unhealthy or unsafe practices. Allow students two or three days to think about their goals before requiring them to complete the forms.

Once students have narrowed in on a long-term goal, ask them to identify two short-term goals related to the long-term goal. For example, if a student's long term goal is to improve physical fitness, short-term goals might include walking or running one mile per day, or working on an exercise bike or treadmill for thirty minutes three days per week.

Discuss with students the importance and value of obtaining support from a close friend, classmate, brother or sister, or parent. These individuals can help them discuss and monitor progress toward their goal and can give them encouragement when they need it. Individuals may want to identify personal rewards or incentives that they can give themselves when they attain each of their short-term goals. Instruct students to keep a daily journal in which they discuss feelings or opinions they have about the progress they are making toward their goal. Ask them to keep a Sunday summary where they discuss their experiences during the week that have helped or hindered advancement toward their goal. They can discuss their successes and failures, help from others, and the appropriateness or difficulty of their goal. The Sunday summary or journal entries can be collected periodically to provide students with feedback and encouragement.

Ask students to submit a final critique that includes a personal evaluation of their program at the end of the six-week period. Encourage them to be as honest as they can with themselves about their results, when they were successful and when they were not, what they thought and felt about their program, and what their future plans for wellness goals might include.

It is useful to tell students that their grade for this exercise will be based on the honesty and thoroughness of their journal, Sunday summaries, and final critique. Grades will not be based on individual success or failure in reaching goals.

Variations

The time period and number of short-term goals can be adapted to meet different classroom schedules.

Source: Barbara Deichl, high school physical education and health teacher.

Feelings Chart

Purpose

This strategy helps students gain a sense of self-awareness and autonomy by encouraging them to identify and label their feelings. It also provides them with an opportunity to choose depictions of their emotions.

TARGET Areas

Authority; Recognition

Grade Level

This strategy is useful in elementary grades.

Procedure

All too often, children are told to negate their feelings with statements like, "Don't cry, you're all right," or "Don't be scared." Through this activity, children learn that feelings are valid and legitimate. They also learn that feelings change.

Using white poster board, create a series of four circle faces that depict the most frequently occurring emotions in younger children (see Figure 2.7). These can be labeled with the words happy, sad, angry, and frustrated. Laminate the faces and tie them together using packing string. Hang the string of four faces in a corner of the classroom.

FIGURE 2.7 Feelings Chart

Happy   Sad   Angry   Frustrated

Write each child's name on a clip clothespin and allow the children to decorate their clothespins with felt markers or crayons.

Introduce the "faces" and discuss the feelings depicted by each face. Ask students to share examples of when they recently felt angry, frustrated, happy, or sad. Then ask each child to clip his or her clothespin to the face that best depicts how he or she feels at that moment. Students may explain why they chose a particular face, but emphasize that they never need to explain why they feel as they do.

Legitimacy is added to the strategy if teachers also make a clothespin and place it on a face. The teachers can then discuss their feelings and how these feelings affect how they act and react. Tell the students that each day when they arrive, they should go to the string of feelings faces and move their clothespin to the face that best describes how they feel that morning. It might also be helpful to encourage the children to discuss how they would like others to treat them when they are angry, frustrated, or sad. Many will say that when they are angry or frustrated, they would like others to leave them alone or give them some "space." When they are sad, they may want others to be more caring; when they are happy, they may want others to share their happiness.

At times, children may display an emotion different from where they placed their clothespin. For example, a child may be smiling broadly as he or she chooses the angry face. This may result from the child choosing a feeling from an experience earlier in the day. It is important, however, to emphasize that feelings are personal and need not be explained.

It is useful for students to discuss how their feelings influence their behavior. For example, when they are angry, they may snap at people for no significant reason. It is also useful to ask the class that if they knew how a person was feeling, would that change the way they might act toward that person? Discuss how students might use the feelings faces to better understand others in the class and how they choose to react to them.

Variations

This strategy can be useful for helping children cope with feeling changes throughout the day. If a child has a disagreement with another student or has been hurt, the teacher might say, "You sound upset. Would it help to change your clothespin?" Simply moving the clothespin from one emotion to another can often help to defuse a situation.

Rather than clothespins and faces, strips of colored paper can be used to represent the different feelings that students experience. Red slips, for example, might be used to convey anger, blue slips to convey sadness, yellow for happiness, etc. A feelings board with small pockets for each student could be made and placed in the front of the room. Students could start each morning by selecting a colored slip that represents their feelings and then place it in their pocket.

Source: Adapted from suggestions by Carol Flora, early childhood teacher; Cindy Bubolz, elementary school teacher.

2.18

Coaching Choices

Purpose

This strategy is designed to foster a sense of autonomy in student athletes by giving them opportunities for self-determination over selected aspects of the daily or weekly practice routines.

TARGET Areas

Task; Authority; Grouping

Grade Level

This strategy can be adapted to almost all grade levels.

Procedure

This strategy offers an opportunity for coaches to give their athletes an opportunity to make decisions regarding aspects of their training and practice schedule. At the first team meeting at the beginning of each season, coaches should tell players that they are responsible for helping to determine the drills needed to learn the skills necessary to become an effective player and a winning team. They are led to believe that their input in acquiring the skills needed to be successful is valued, appreciated, and expected.

After the team has been practicing for several weeks and the players have acquired a solid foundation of skills and conditioning, the team captains are asked to help determine the practice schedule for the coming week. They are encouraged to solicit the opinions of the ball players from various positions and to use these ideas to help the coaches determine the week's practice schedule.

All team members are encouraged to volunteer their suggestions regarding the practice schedule to the team captains or to the coaches. This allows all team members to contribute their personal insights into what team and individual skills require additional or supplementary work, and allows players to work on skills that they know need more repetition to achieve the unconscious competence level that is required to consistently perform the skill during the heat of competition. Players also develop a strong sense of ownership for using practices to developing their individual skills to the highest level possible.

It is important to help all team members believe that their ideas are valued and important to the coaches' efforts to use practice time as effectively as possible. When students believe that they have some control over their practice schedule, they are less likely to try to avoid drills or to "dog" it when the coaches are not looking.

Variations

Some coaches may prefer to give captains a greater role in deciding practice schedules. This is especially important if team members are expected to work on conditioning and other skills during the preseason. If captains are seen as individuals who convey players' opinions to the coaches, the players will be more willing to follow their leadership during the off season.

Source: Torrence Acheson, softball coach.

Voting with Your Feet

Purpose

This strategy builds autonomy by enabling students to actively express an opinion on an issue without verbalizing it. It is a useful icebreaker early in the school year. It can also be used to strengthen listening and comprehension skills in foreign language classes.

TARGET Areas

Task; Grouping; Evaluation

Grade Level

This strategy can be adapted to almost all grade levels and content areas; it is especially useful in foreign language classes.

Procedure

Before using this activity, make three signs with the words *no, yes,* and *no comment* written in large block letters. Laminating the signs will increase their durability. Place each sign on a different wall of your classroom before the students arrive.

Instruct students that you are going to ask them an opinion question from their reading or from the material they have been studying. After they hear the question, they are required to get up from their desks and stand under the sign that best expresses their answer to the question.

Once all of the students are standing under the sign that expresses their opinion, ask them to discuss some of the reasons that influenced their choice. After a few minutes, call on two or three students from each group to share their reasons. When each group has had a chance to express some of their reasons, ask the students to return to their seats. You can then continue with the discussion of the opinion question or switch to another lesson or topic.

Depending on the skill level of the students, foreign language classes can be encouraged to conduct their discussion in the language being studied.

Variations

There may be a tendency for students to quickly choose the *no comment* sign when the discussion is being conducted in a foreign language. Teachers can encourage students to listen carefully so that they can make a decision. If this strategy is going to be used for several opinion questions throughout the course, they may want to limit students to using the *no comment* answer once or twice a quarter.

Source: Jamie Gurholt, Spanish teacher.

2.20

Teacher-Advisor Program

Purpose

This strategy supports student autonomy and self-determination with a teacher-advisor program that encourages students to do an academic self-evaluation and to monitor and select academic and behavioral-social goals.

TARGET Areas

Task; Authority

Grade Level

This strategy is useful for upper elementary, middle, and high school.

Procedure

After students receive their progress reports in the middle of each quarter, a teacher-advisor program can help them take a serious look at how they are doing. This activity helps students realize that they are in control of their successes and failures, and that the quarter outcomes depend on their actions. Through self-evaluation and individual goal setting, students can choose to maintain or improve their academic and behavioral-social outcomes. Involving students in self-evaluation provides them with an opportunity to understand their academic performance better and to experience a sense of personal responsibility. When students evaluate and record their goals, they are more likely to develop an internal locus of control and to accept a relationship between their efforts and outcomes. Similarly, self-evaluation enables students to identify academic and behavioral-social areas that may need improvement.

One approach to a teacher-advisor program is to encourage homeroom teachers to become advisors for their homeroom students. Through this process, homeroom teacher-advisors can help students conduct self-evaluations and establish and monitor their academic and behavioral goals.

Starting on the first day after midterm progress reports, homeroom teachers distribute a Self-Evaluation and Goal Planning Sheet similar to the one in Figure 2.8 for each course that the student is taking. Discuss the sheet and encourage students to use the form to help them think about and select one academic goal and one behavioral/social goal they wish to accomplish in each course before the end of the quarter.

During the next three or four days, homeroom teacher-advisors confer individually with each student to discuss their Self-Evaluation and Goal Planning Sheets and helping them clarify or, if necessary, revise their goals and time lines. It is important that the teacher-advisors avoid pressuring students or choosing goals for them. Rather, the teacher-advisors focus on being good listeners and on encouraging students to assume the responsibility for their own choices.

Experience shows that students are quite capable of setting goals but they need some guidance in selecting specific and achievable goals. For example, many students mention that to improve in a course, the need "to study better." The teacher-advisor can help these students clarify the meaning of "to study better." The advisor might ask the student questions related to note taking, reviewing notes, reading and rereading the text, seeking help from the subject teacher before or after school, and so on. These specific questions can help students narrow their focus and establish specific and achievable goals.

The advisor can also help students evaluate the probability of achieving their goals. A student who is struggling in a course and is receiving an F may be unrealistic in expecting to earn an A by the end of the quarter. The teacher-advisor's job is to encourage effort, improvement, and realistic achievement—elements that can promote positive attitudes and success. When students are setting themselves up for failure, the teacher-advisor can ask the student how much time he or she is willing to devote to this goal and if the expected outcome seems realistic. If students insist on setting unrealistic goals, they may feel a sense of hopelessness or be unwilling to accept a less than successful performance. (See Raffini, 1993, chapter 2, for a discussion of failure-avoidance behavior and the tendency of some students to establish unrealistic goals to protect their sense of self-worth.)

FIGURE 2.8   Self-Evaluation and Goal Planning Sheet

Name _____   Advisor _____

Subject _____   Quarter _____

1. **Self-Evaluation:**

   a. How am I doing in this course? _____

   _____

   b. What difficulties have I been having? _____

   _____

   c. How much time and effort having I been spending in this course? _____

   _____

   d. Do I need more help in this course? _____ If yes, how have I tried to

   get it? _____

2. **Academic Goal**

   a. My goal to achieve before the end of the quarter is _____

   _____

   b. I want to work on this goal because _____

   _____

   c. I will achieve this goal by _____

   _____

3. **Behavior or Social Goal**

   a. My goal to achieve before the end of the quarter is _____

   _____

   b. I want to work on this goal because _____

   _____

   c. I will achieve this goal by _____

   _____

Variations

Advisors may choose to use this activity at the beginning of each quarter and adapt self-evaluation and goal planning sheets to specific grade levels. Follow-up conferences are also useful for helping students evaluate their plans.

Source: Adapted from Lora Westra, middle school teacher, and Oak Creek-Franklin, WI School District.

CHAPTER THREE

Strategies for Enhancing Competence in All Students

To increase the intrinsic motivation of *all* students, it is necessary to create an environment in which students can discover that their serious effort toward learning makes it possible for them to attain a sense of academic competence. Although the amount of time and effort required for academic achievement varies considerably among students, they all need to have access to the feelings of competence that comes from achievement.

RECOMMENDATIONS FOR ENHANCING COMPETENCE FOR ALL STUDENTS

1. *Evaluate achievement against the attainment of clearly stated instructional objectives.* If all students are to experience academic success, they need to know exactly what knowledge and skills they are required to master.

2. *Wherever possible, achievement should be the constant and time the variable.* Many classrooms provide all students with the same amount of time to master learning objectives. Because some students learn at faster rates than others, it seems advisable to allow slower-learning students the time they need to attain the same level of content mastery as faster-learning students.

3. *Use individual goal-setting strategies to allow students to define their own criteria for success.* Allowing students the opportunity to decide their own task and content goals empowers them to define their own standard for success. This enables them to raise or lower their goals relative to their current skills.

4. *After initial instruction, use formative tests to identify the specific objectives not yet mastered by each student.* Students vary in the amount of time each requires to master the instructional objectives. Slower-learning students are likely to require more time and additional instruction. Using diagnostic tests ensures that each set of learning tasks is thoroughly mastered before subsequent tasks are inaugurated.

5. *Use criterion-referenced rather than norm-referenced evaluation procedures to determine student grades.* Specific standards of excellence can and should be identified by teachers. It is then necessary to evaluate students against these standards, rather than against the performance of others.

6. *Allow students to retake, without a penalty, parallel forms of exams that cover clearly stated objectives.* Although difficult to implement, this recommendation assures students that increased effort can lead to higher levels of success.

7. *Design learning and evaluation activities so that performance outcomes are related to the level of effort expended.* To ensure effort-outcome dependence, teachers must structure learning tasks so that students' meaningful and reasonable efforts are reinforced by goal attainment.

8. *Match learning tasks and the pace of learning to the skill level of individual students.* Instructional objectives need to be task-analyzed to ensure that each student is working at a task appropriate to his or her skill level.

9. *Provide faster-learning students with challenging opportunities to enrich and extend their content mastery.* Intrinsic motivation requires that all students experience self-determined challenges.

10. *Design assessment procedures that do not restrict high grades to faster learning students.* High standards are desirable and necessary; their attainment, however, should not be artificially limited or restricted to faster-learning students.

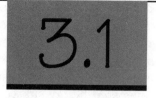

Know-Want-Learned Listing

Purpose

This strategy uses three nonthreatening brainstorming activities to encourage students to become actively involved in new topics. Adaptable to any content area, the activity builds group relatedness while allowing all students to experience competence.

TARGET Areas

Task; Grouping: Evaluation

Grade Level

This strategy can be adapted to all grade levels and content areas.

Procedure

When introducing a new instructional topic, the teacher encourages the students to generate a list of things that they already know about the topic. The teacher or a designated student can record this list of things *Known* on the chalkboard or on an overhead. Since this is a brainstorming activity, the group should try to identify as many things as possible that they know about the topic without spending too much time discussing each idea. After the list is completed (allow approximately ten minutes for this), the group can discuss the validity of each item and temporarily remove those that lack consensus.

A second brainstorming activity encourages the class to list all of the things that they *Want to Learn* about the topic. Again, the teacher or a designated student should keep a record of these ideas on the chalkboard or overhead. Information questioned on the *Known* list can be placed on the *Want to Learn* list.

It is useful to keep both lists posted in the classroom so that the teacher and students can refer to them during the unit. It is especially useful to use the *Want to Learn* list to monitor the class's progress in accomplishing their goals for the unit.

At the completion of the unit, the brainstorming activity is again used to generate a third list of information about the topic that the students learned during the unit. This *Learned* list should contain only those things that were not included on the *Know* and *Want to Learn* lists. The *Learned* list is an especially useful unit review activity.

Students in Mrs. Trapp's second-grade class at Maywood Elementary School, Monona Grove, WI construct a Know, Want, Learned Listing

Variations

This strategy may be more effective if used in a cooperative learning groups format. Small groups of students can generate their own lists of *Know* or *Want to Learn* information about the topic, or some groups can work on one list while other groups work on a different list. Have a group recorder report the results of each group's production to produce detailed *Know, Want to Learn,* and *Learned* lists for the entire class.

The lists could be generated in any combination of small and large groups. For example, the *Know* list might be generated during a discussion of the entire class and the *Want to Learn* and *Learned* lists could be used as small group activities.

Students could be encouraged to keep their own *Want to Learn* and *Learned* lists and add to the lists as they progress through the unit. With younger students, the lists could be used for a bulletin board display or as part of a personal portfolio.

Source: Adapted by Barbara Trapp, elementary school teacher.

The Unwritten Dialogue

Purpose

This activity is designed to enhance student competence in critical analysis of a literary work and in oral expression. It also stimulates student enjoyment of reading and writing.

TARGET Areas

Task; Authority; Grouping; Evaluation

Grade Level

This strategy is especially suited to middle school students, but it can be used effectively in grades four through twelve.

Procedure

After reading a novel or assigned chapters from a book, ask students to think about the sequence of story events and to reflect on the dialogues between various characters that reveal important information to the reader. Next, ask students to think about important story events for which no dialogue was written. Could they, as readers, *imagine* the dialogue that took place at these points in the story? After brainstorming scenes that did not have dialogue, students can be challenged to choose a scene and to write the unwritten conversation that might have taken place. Students should be encouraged to write their dialogues to fit the facts of the story. When they are finished, the teacher should divide the class into small groups and each group member should read his or her dialogue to the others. Then the authors become actors and rehearse their dialogues for presentation to the class.

Depending on the time available, one, two, or all of the dialogues can be presented. Students should act in their own dialogues and take a role in the dialogue of others. The group should decide which dialogues will be presented and who will play each role. It is important, however, to encourage the group to share the roles equally.

Variations

Students can be encouraged to dress appropriately for the roles and to make or bring small props to enhance their presentations. The teacher may want to collect the dialogues for individual evaluation, but the class could conduct a mock Academy Awards presentation, using a secret ballot, to determine nominations and awards for "Best Script," "Best Male or Female Actor," "Best Supporting Role," and so on.

As a lead-up to the activity, the tacher could ask students to simply find a dialogue in the book that they would like to learn and present. Another variation would be to have students work independently to write a monologue involving a main character's thoughts as he or she reflects on some conflict within the story. Students might also write a monologue in which a character steps outside the real story to explain his or her reasons for handling a problem or conflict in a particular way.

This strategy could be modified for use in science or social studies classes. Students could write dialogues for famous individuals at critical points in their lives or relate what they were thinking when they made famous discoveries.

Source: Katy Grogan, middle school English teacher.

Estimating Esquire

Purpose

This strategy is designed to enhance the feelings of success and competence in all students.

TARGET Areas

Task; Recognition

Grade Level

This strategy can be adapted to almost all grade levels at which mathematical estimating and reasoning are important objectives.

Procedure

Completely fill a clear plastic jar with an object of your choice (e.g., peanuts, marshmallows, dry macaroni noodles, dry cereal). Throughout the week, allow students to make one estimate per day of how many objects they believe are in the jar. At the end of the week, the true amount is revealed and the estimates compared to the actual amount. The student who comes the closest to the total is given the title of Estimating Esquire for the following week. He or she can be given a special certificate and is responsible for filling the jar and helping to read and record estimates for the following week. The teacher might want to send a letter home, similar to the one that follows, to explain the duties of the Estimating Esquire.

> *Dear Mr. and Mrs. _____ ,*
>
> *I am pleased to report that _____ has been selected as our Estimating Esquire for the coming week. Each child in our class has an opportunity to make a daily estimate of how many objects are in our estimating jar, and your child's estimate was the closest to the actual number.*
>
> *A responsibility of our weekly Estimating Esquire is to find objects to fill the jar for the following week. I hope that over the weekend you can help your child find an object to fill the jar so that he can return it Monday. A variety of objects of identical size can be used. In the past we have used things like peanuts, marshmallows, dry macaroni noodles, dry cereal, dry beans, Styrofoam packing nuggets, marbles, and identical-size toy blocks.*
>
> *Mathematical estimation and reasoning are important objectives in our class, and we appreciate any help you can give your child to maintain our estimating activity. Thank you for your continued support.*
>
> *Sincerely,*

All students are encouraged to chart the difference between their estimations and the actual number in the jar on individual graphs. The teacher should avoid discussing the chart for the first few weeks. After the third or fourth week, students can discuss how they are doing at the task, and should be encouraged to explain the reasoning that they are using to make their estimates. The teacher can then discuss the different sizes and shapes of the objects and how the students might use past numbers to increase their accuracy at estimation.

Variations

For younger students, it may be useful to use more than one jar per week so that more Estimating Esquires can be identified. For an added challenge, change the shape of the jar or fill two different-shapped jars with the same objects and compare results. Older students might convert the difference between their estimations and the actual number to a percentage and then chart their accuracy percentage.

Source: Adapted by Pam Sternad, fourth grade teacher.

Graphic Note Taking

Purpose

The purpose of this activity is to develop student competence in note-taking skills while enhancing their sense of autonomy and creativity.

TARGET Areas

Task; Authority; Evaluation

Grade Level

This strategy is well suited to middle school students; at these grade levels, students are often not skilled in note-taking and yet are encountering challenging reading and lecture material.

Procedure

Tell students that they are going to learn a new way to take notes from reading material or from teacher presentations. Rather than using a traditional outline or writing as much as they can about what was read or said, they should try to capture the main ideas in picture form. When using graphic note-taking they should divide their notepaper into four sections, using a different section for each major topic (one sheet will allow for eight topics). When using graphic note-taking, students should try to draw simple symbols and objects to trigger their memory of what they are reading or hearing. Reassure students that the objective of the activity is not to be artistic, but to find a graphic way to quickly get the important ideas on paper. The teacher may find it useful to prepare examples similar to those in Figure 3.1 to demonstrate this new form of note-taking.

The teacher should then assign a short selection of reading for the class to practice their graphic note-taking skills. When they are finished, the teacher can encourage students to explain their drawings to each other in small groups. They usually enjoy comparing their illustrations, and this process helps students expand their understanding of the key ideas in the reading. After further practice, students should be encouraged to evaluate whether this method of note-taking is effective for them.

Variations

Students could be assigned to work alone or in small groups to develop an outline of the material using their graphic notes. The teacher might also choose to allow the use of graphic notes on a future test.

Source: Adapted from Katy Grogan and Jim Rotar middle school teachers.

FIGURE 3.1   Graphic Notes on Japan

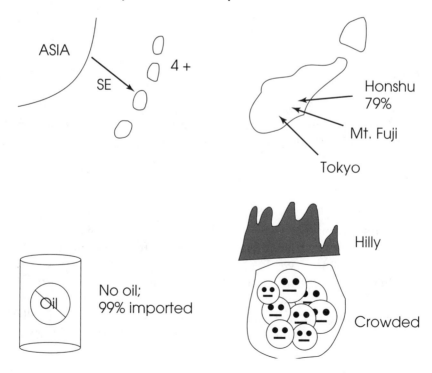

3.5

Reflective Participation for Everyone

Purpose

This strategy builds competence and relatedness by allowing all students a chance to contribute to class discussions. It is also useful for reducing attention-seeking hand-raising, common in many elementary classrooms.

TARGET Areas

Recognition; Evaluation; Time

Grade Level

This strategy can be adapted to almost all grade levels and content areas.

Procedure

Attention-seeking hand-raising is common in many classrooms. It is most evident when students raise their hands to offer answers before questions are asked. Shy students are often pushed aside by their more aggressive classmates who frequently dominate class discussions. This strategy eliminates hand-raising from discussions and substitutes a procedure that encourages all students to participate.

The teacher begins by writing each student's name on a three by five card and then assigns each student to a discussion partner. Depending on the maturity of the group, partner selection can be accomplished by the teacher assigning partners using the random grouping procedure discussed in strategy 4.6, or allowing students to choose partners. Students are asked to sit next to their partners during all class discussions.

The teacher begins the discussion by asking a question or seeking an opinion on the topic to be discussed. The teacher then asks students to spend about fifteen seconds *thinking* about their response. Next, the class is asked to quietly *share* their response with their partner, each taking about thirty seconds. Finally, the teacher calls on a student selected from the shuffled stack of three by five cards to *share* his or her answer or opinion. If the student seems unsure or reluctant to answer, the teacher should avoid calling on another student to assist (the hand-raisers will want to jump in here). Instead, the teacher should encourage this student to formulate a response by offering a hint or giving a choice from alternatives. Shy students, especially, benefit from the teacher's prompting since they often need a little more time and support before venturing a response.

When the first student has finished with his or her response, the teacher uses the card stack to select two or three additional students to contribute to the discussion. When finished with a card, the teacher should return it to the middle of the stack and shuffle the stack often. Thus, all students will have an equal chance to be selected. After most ideas and opinions have been expressed, the teacher can ask the class if anyone has something to add that has not already been said. It is only at this point that hand-raising is allowed. The teacher should make sure that only *new* ideas or opinions are offered.

Variations

For each discussion topic, the teacher may want to place selected cards on the bottom of the deck and draw new cards from the top. This will ensure that all students have a chance to contribute once before others are selected a second time. Teachers can also vary the method of partner assignment, sometimes using random pairs, student choice, or teacher selection.

Source: Suggested by Janice Collins, middle school English teacher.

3.6

Choral Poetry

Purpose

This strategy is designed to help students develop a sense of competence in writing poetry and stimulate their enjoyment of poetry as a form of self-expression. The strategy also builds a sense of group relatedness by encouraging students to work with others in the class.

TARGET Areas

Task; Authority; Recognition; Grouping

Grade Level

This strategy is especially useful for middle and high school language arts or English classes.

Procedure

Many students enjoy reading or listening to poetry, but most have feelings of insecurity when they are asked to write a poem. As part of a poetry unit or as part of a literature unit that explores man's relationship with nature, the teacher and a willing volunteer (student or adult) perform a choral poetry reading for the class using one or two nature poems from Paul Fleischman's *Joyful Noise: Poems in Two Voices* (1988; available in many school libraries or from interlibrary loan).

After a class discussion of the meaning and the special structure of these poems, students are asked to work with a partner to choose a dramatic choral reading from this collection for the class. When all poems have been presented, the students are encouraged to work with a partner and write their own choral poem. Topics that work well include those that explore two opposing characteristics of a subject (a poem that argues that cats are wonderful/horrible pets) or two subjects that share some characteristics but also share important contrasts (a poem about dogs and cats). Depending on the focus of the language arts unit, students could be asked to choose a topic related to nature, sports, people, or story themes or characters.

A collection of high-interest choral poems suitable to the grade level of the students is needed for this activity. The previously mentioned Fleischman book provides an excellent source with a nature theme. Another source is *I Am Phoenix*, from the same author and publisher.

Variations

Teachers can challenge students to work in larger groups to write poems for three, four, or more voices, depending on the topic. The choral writing activity could also be adapted for use in other subject areas such as science or social studies where students are studying similarities and contrasts of issues or topics.

Source: Suggested by Katy Grogan, middle school teacher and Karen Halverson, high school English teacher.

3.7

Math Mind Reading

Purpose

This strategy can enable all students to experience a sense of competence and relatedness. It also can stimulate student interest and involving with learning math.

TARGET Areas

Task; Grouping; Evaluation

Grade Level

This strategy is especially useful for upper elementary, middle, and high school.

Procedure

Only basic arithmetic skills are required for students to be successful in this activity. However, analyzing the activity provides practice in basic algebra skills.

The teacher starts by asking students to perform the following eight mental operations:

1. Think of a number (preferably between 1 and 10 to simplify the mental math)
2. Multiply by 5
3. Add 10
4. Add the original number
5. Subtract 4
6. Divide by 6
7. Add 3
8. Subtract the original number

The teacher now announces to the class that he or she can read each student's mind—they are all thinking of the number four. (The teacher can repeat the statements if some students have made an error in calculation.)

To analyze the process, the teacher repeats the statements and asks students to use X as their original number and to write down the corresponding algebraic expression for each operation. Their list should look like the following:

Statement	Algebraic Expression
1. Think of a number	X
2. Multiply by 5	$5X$
3. Add 10	$5X + 10$
4. Add the original number	$6X + 10$
5. Subtract 4	$6X + 6$
6. Divide by 6	$X + 1$
7. Add 3	$X + 4$
8. Subtract the original number	4

Students can now work with a partner or in a small group to make up their own math mind-reading device. They should have at least six steps and should write down the English statements in a column on the left side of their paper and the corresponding algebraic statement on the right side. They will avoid some difficulties if they add or multiply for the first two or three steps.

When they complete the task, they should practice on each other to see if the trick works. If it does not, they should examine the algebra column and work cooperatively to see where the mistake or mistakes occurred.

Variations

Instead of math mind-reading devices that finish with a predetermined number, students could construct devices that end with the same number as the one originally selected. The following is an example of such a device:

1. Think of a number	X
2. Add 10	$X + 10$
3. Multiply by 2	$2X + 20$
4. Add 5	$2X + 25$
5. Subtract 3	$2X + 22$
6. Add the original number	$3X + 22$
7. Add 5	$3X + 27$
8. Divide by 3	$X + 9$
9. Subtract 9	X

As added algebra practice, the teacher could give students several examples of English statements and ask students to construct algebraic equivalents.

Source: Richard Hall, high school math teacher; Brown, Smith, & Dolciani (1983). *Basic algebra.* New York: Houghton Mifflin.

Crossnumber Puzzle

Purpose

This strategy can build problem-solving skills while stimulating student interest and enjoyment with numbers. It can also help students feel successful.

Target Areas

Task; Autonomy; Evaluation; Time

Grade Level

This strategy can be used in upper elementary, middle, and high school.

Procedure

This problem is like a crossword puzzle except it involves numbers. The first clue is given and from that clue students are encouraged to complete the remainder of the puzzle. Numbers range from three to five digits and each number is used only once. (Students will find it helpful to cross out each number when it is used.) An example of a crossnumber puzzle is given in Figure 3.2.

This strategy builds concentration and problem-solving skills. It is useful during transition times or when students have finished their other assignments.

FIGURE 3.2 Crossnumbers

3 Digit Numbers

251
749
938
415
349

4 Digit Numbers

2890
3279
7257
6928
9664
2929
6247
2588
8149

5 Digit Numbers

27460
72662
31762
27543
45791
96583
42790
17534
40263
85238
92172
83372
63370
66529
54762

6 Digit Numbers

985266
362213
792312
547622
305178
274428
370822
169357
369329
274013
176076

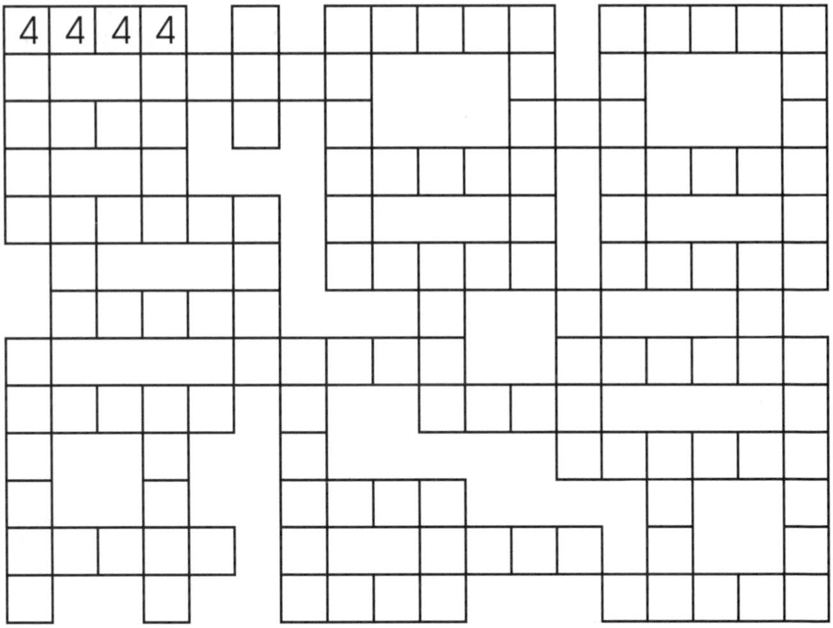

Solution

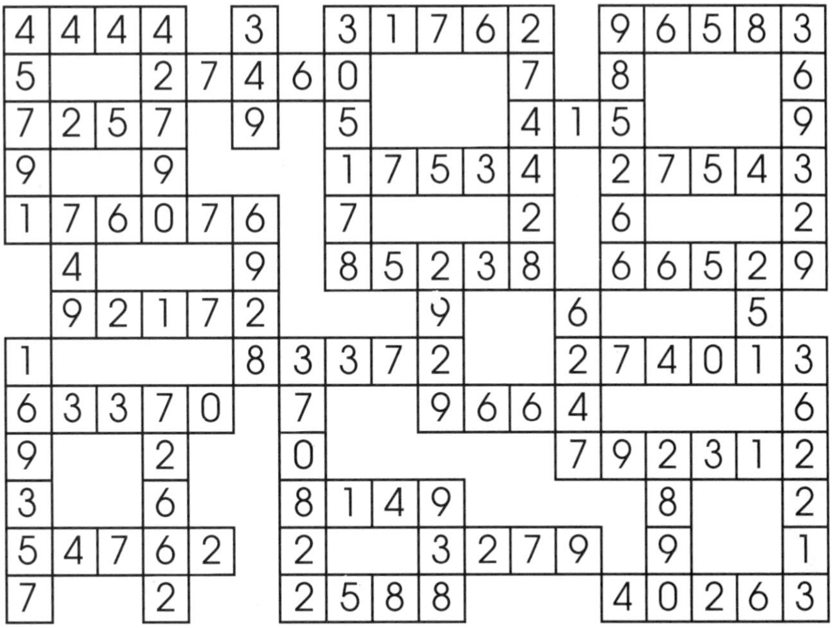

Variations

Students can be encouraged to construct their own crossnumber puzzles on graph paper. They should be careful to ensure that there is only one correct solution to the puzzle.

Source: Richard Hall, high school math teacher; *Word games for puzzle lovers.* (1989). Norwalk, CT: Denny Press.

3.9

Seeing with the Mind's Eye

Purpose

This strategy enhances competence by using visualization to enable students to gain a deeper understanding of curricular content. It can also help students experience a sense of autonomy as they create their individual perceptions of an event.

TARGET Areas

Task; Authority; Evaluation

Grade Level

This strategy can be adapted to all grade levels.

Procedure

This strategy takes students on a guided visualization of a specific curricular incident. It requires that students have previously developed a sense of trust that the teacher will not embarrass or frighten them. The teacher starts by reviewing the unit content to find some critical incident or relationship that is important to understanding the unit objectives. It is this incident that the teacher wants to help students see with the mind's eye.

The teacher begins the visualization by asking students to sit comfortably and to keep their eyes closed so that they can see more clearly with their mind. They should try to relax and take deep comfortable breaths. With each exhale they should try to relax more completely and release any tension they may be experiencing. Encourage students to take an inventory of their bodies, starting with their toes and working up to their heads. If they experience tension in any part of their body, they should tighten up the muscles in that area for a few seconds and then slowly release the tension as they relax their muscles and exhale. It should take about one or two minutes to get the class relaxed.

Once the students are physically relaxed, ask them to try to visualize the focus object or incident. In a social studies unit on the Civil War, for example, the students might try to recreate in their mind's eye an important battle, or they might want to visualize seeing a family member who has decided to fight for the other side. In a science unit, students might want to visualize the circulatory system through the eyes of a single blood cell, or they might want to be a neuron or a blade of grass. Language arts and English classes might want to see a particular scene from a book through the eyes of a main character.

Teachers may want to write out the script ahead of time so that the students are not distracted during the visualization. All that is required is a rich and descriptive vocabulary and a slow pace so that students can "see" what the teacher describes. The slow, steady pacing also enables students to create their own details and images. In addition to sight, teachers can also encourage their students to smell certain odors, experience certain tastes, or hear specific sounds during their visualizations. Since visualizations are uniquely personal, it is important to tell students that they are in total control of the process; if they feel uncomfortable or anxious with an image, they should leave it and focus on something more pleasant.

At the conclusion of the visualization, the teacher should ask students to slowly open their eyes and return to the class. It is important to allow enough time for students to discuss their experiences during the visualization. Teachers might ask students to write a few sentences describing what they viewed before the discussion begins.

When first using this strategy, teachers should keep the visualizations under five minutes and should focus on concrete and nonpersonal images. As a learning tool, visualization can help students gain a clearer and more personal understanding of curricular content.

Variations

Following the visualization, teachers might ask students to discuss their experiences with partners or in small groups before conducting a large group discussion. This should enable more students to share their experience with others.

As students become comfortable with visualization, the teacher can use more open-ended exercises. Depending on the maturity of the students, personal experiences can often be used to better understand the curricular content. For example, asking students to recall a time when they were lost might help them better appreciate map-reading skills.

3.10

The Teaching Assistant

Purpose

This strategy provides all students with a sense of competence by helping the teacher with the responsibilities of a working classroom.

TARGET Areas

Recognition

Grade Level

This strategy is especially appropriate for elementary and middle schools, but can be adapted to all levels.

Procedure

On each Monday of the school year, the teacher randomly selects one student to become the class teaching assistant (T.A.) for the week. Since most elementary teachers have fewer students than there are weeks in the school year, students are not allowed to repeat as T.A. until all students have been selected once. The teaching assistant can be given many assignments that help the teacher with classroom procedures while providing the T.A. with an opportunity to practice responsibility. These assignments should be written on a permanent poster and explained to the class at the beginning of the year. After the first couple of weeks, student will usually undertake their responsibilities with little direction or explanation from the teacher. Assignments might include the following:

1. Copy daily assignments into the teacher's notebook at the end of the day
2. Write short "We Missed You" cards to be placed in the desks of students who are absent
3. Ensure that a copy of daily assignments are placed in the desks of absent students
4. Take attendance
5. Collect and count lunch or milk money
6. Help set up and run audio-visual equipment needed throughout the week
7. Have a "working lunch" with the teacher to discuss the weekly assignments and schedule
8. High school science or performance classes can use the T.A. to help set up equipment for experiments or demonstrations

Some teachers find it helpful to have a special desk near the teacher's desk that can be reserved for the weekly T.A. Attendance and assignment sheets, "Missed You" cards, and other forms likely to be sued by the T.A. can be kept in this desk. Although the "working lunch" may be a bit of a hassle for the teacher, it can be special enough to create an indelible memory for many students.

Variations

The teaching assistant's responsibilities will vary according to the age of the students and the structure of the classroom. It may be useful near the beginning of the year to brainstorm with the class other possible T.A. responsibilities and tasks. A small certificate or token of appreciation could be presented to the student at the end of the week.

The T.A. assignment can be lengthened or shortened according to the number of students in the class.

Source: Jeri Koss, elementary school teacher.

3.11

Success Contract

Purpose

This strategy supports feelings of competence in all students by enabling them to experience effort-outcome dependence in the grading process.

TARGET Areas

Task; Evaluation; Time

Grade Level

This strategy can be adapted to all grade levels and content areas that evaluate student performance with letter grades.

Procedure

Prepare a grade contract that guarantees students an A or B for the semester if they fulfill the contract provisions (see Figure 3.3). Distribute the grade contract and inform students that for the next grading period they can continue to be evaluated by the established grading procedure for the class or they can choose to sign the guaranteed grade contract. Students who sign the contract are expected to complete assignments to a level of quality established by the teacher for the grades of A or B. If their work does not meet these quality standards they must revise their assignments until they do. During tests, contract students must demonstrate mastery at the A or B level or agree to participate in study groups outside of class

FIGURE 3.3   Grade Contract Guaranteed A or B

PROVISIONS:

I promise to hand in only quality work for this grading period. Homework, projects, and tests will only be accepted if they are of A or B quality. I agree to resubmit work until it meets the teacher's A or B standard. If I do not meet the A or B standard on an exam, I will participate in outside-of-class study groups, reteaching sessions, or tutorial exercises in order to demonstrate mastery on a parallel retest. I understand that all work for the grading period must be completed to the A or B standard and that unfinished assignments will not be accepted.

If I sign this contract, I realize that I will only receive the grade of A, B, Incomplete, or F for this grading period. I realize that an F will not be given without an Incomplete given first, and I will be given every available chance to complete my work for the grading period.

Student Signature _____   Date _____

Parent Signature _____   Date _____

As your teacher, I agree to meet individually with you to discuss your progress, to ensure that test questions measure clearly stated course or unit objectives that have been made available to you, and will be willing to work with you outside of class. In short, I will only accept quality work, and I will do my best to help you succeed.

Teacher Signature _____   Date _____

time, attend reteaching sessions, or work on tutorial exercises until they can display mastery on a parallel retest.

As part of the contract, the teacher promises to meet individually with students to discuss their progress, to ensure that test questions measure clearly stated course or unit objectives that have been distributed to students, and to work with students outside of class time.

Students who sign the contract will receive as much time as possible to complete their obligation. The teacher agrees to avoid giving a failing grade without first giving an incomplete grade, and students are given every available chance to make up the incomplete grade.

The teacher can make contracts available for each grading period. Having both students and parents sign the contract provides for parental involvement and communication.

Variations

Some teachers may find it difficult to maintain two separate grading systems during the same grading period. Instead, they may want to design the success contract for use with all students during a particular grading period. Retake exams are often difficult to schedule. It may be necessary for students to give up some of their out-of-school time for this purpose.

Source: Harold Beedle, middle school social studies teacher.

3.12

Word Sort

Purpose

This strategy builds a sense of competence and relatedness through a group activity that can help all students improve their comprehension of content reading.

TARGET Areas

Task; Authority

Grade Level

This strategy can be adapted to almost all grade levels and content areas.

Procedure

This strategy helps students improve their understanding and comprehension of textbook and supplementary reading selections by encouraging them to use categories to organize and classify information. Through this inductive process, students gain practice integrating the meaning of words.

The teacher begins by reviewing the assigned reading selection to decide what information is important enough for all students to integrate. Words representing this information are then placed into a word sort that require students to use categories to identify and classify the shared features of the words. In addition to selecting the important words, the teacher also predetermines the categories to be used in classification by examining the selected passage to identify inclusive concepts.

Next, the teacher assigns students to small groups and distributes the words and categories (chalkboards and overheads can be used). The teacher then asks students to study the reading selection to identify features that the words have in common and to sort the words into the predetermined categories. Students are asked to discuss the meanings of the words and to seek consensus before they place the words into categories. They should also be prepared to justify their decisions based on the information contained in the story.

The following list is an example of a word sort taken from a social studies unit (Wham, 1988, p. 54). The teacher asks students to discuss the words and to use the reading selection to sort the words into the appropriate categories. Next, the teacher should tell the students that some words can be sorted into more than one category, but it is important that each student can explain the reasons for their category selections.

Categories

Natural Resources

Human Resources

Capital Resources

Words to Sort

tools	machinery	tractors
minerals	trees	typewriters
water	wildlife	power plants
labor	factories	buildings

Variations

This word sort could be done individually and the results shared in small groups. This might give all students a chance to benefit from the classification process before starting the group discussion. Students can also be encouraged to discover additional categories for sorting the words. After they have had practice with word sorts, students can be asked to develop their own lists of words and categories that others can use when reading from their text.

Source: Wham, M. A. (Spring, 1988). *Three strategies for content area teachers.* Illinois Reading Council Journal, *16*(1), pp. 52–55.

3.13

Synectics

Purpose

This strategy uses a creative thinking process to increase students' sense of competence at understanding academic content and problem solving. Since this is a group activity without right or wrong answers, it can also help students satisfy their needs for autonomy and relatedness.

TARGET Areas

Task; Authority; Grouping; Evaluation

Grade Level

This strategy can be adapted to upper elementary, middle, and high school levels in almost all content areas.

Procedure

Synectics refers to an eight-step metaphorical process that brings together disparate elements or ideas that can help students expand their creative thinking skills. These skills may be used to better understand academic content or they can be focused on discovering creative solutions to common problems.

Prior to conducting a classroom synectics activity, teachers should ensure that they have established a climate of trust and acceptance. Students will be asked to share ideas that may, upon first examination, appear foolish or unrelated. Feeling safe enough to take this risk is only possible when others are willing to suspend judgment and criticism. Creating a psychologically safe classroom environment does not happen without practice. Students need prior experiences with brainstorming and open-ended discussions before they undertake a synectics activity.

The following steps identify the synectics process (Clasen & Clasen, 1993):

1. The teacher presents a problem or idea.
2. The class clarifies the problem or idea.
3. The teacher asks the class to brainstorm *direct analogies* or comparisons that have similar characteristics to the problem. All are recorded on the chalk board or overhead. This step is akin to "making the familiar strange."
4. From the list of direct analogies the class chooses one to examine more closely. The teacher then asks participants to close their eyes and imagine being the analogy. This *personal analogy* is akin to "making the strange familiar."
5. Following the personal analogy, the teacher asks the class to describe what it felt like being the analogy chosen. This list of descriptions and feelings is recorded on the chalkboard or overhead. When each student has had a chance to offer a description or feeling, the teacher then encourages students to examine the list to identify contradictory elements that may have emerged (these pairs of words may be circled or numbered). These pairs of contradictory elements represent a *compressed conflict,* or a forced fit between seemingly polar opposite attributes.
6. From the list of compressed conflicts, the class chooses one to examine more closely. The teacher asks students to again close their eyes and imagine a *new direct analogy* that represents both polar opposite attributes.
7. The teacher asks students to describe their new analogy and how it maintained opposite characteristics. The teacher records the new analogies on the chalkboard and students attempt to force fit all of the ideas presented during the synectics exercise into a solution to the problem or the development of a new way of looking at the original problem.
8. Students discuss their opinions and feelings regarding the synectics exercise.

The following two examples from Clasen and Clasen (1993, pp 134–136) demonstrate how teachers might use a synectics exercise in an elementary and secondary classroom.

Example 1—Problem Solving in an Elementary Classroom

Step 1: The Problem Presented

Things are not going well on the playground

Step 2: The Problem Clarified

Older kids are too bossy

Too much fighting

Certain kids pick on others

Some equipment always taken over by a few

Step 3: Direct Analogy

The teacher asks children to form direct comparisons between the playground and another animate or inanimate thing (making the familiar strange).

A jungle

A zoo

A battlefield

A runaway truck

A broken record player

Early American colonies

A pet store where all the pets get loose

All examples are listed. After listing, children may ask for clarification of any example, or they may discuss each idea briefly.

Step 4: Personal Analogy

The teacher may ask the students to select one of the direct analogies to study more closely. (Or the teacher may select the analogy to be used.) Next, the teacher asks students "to become the thing." This is often done as a visualization experience (making the strange familiar).

For example, students may select to become the animals loose in the pet store. Students play the part of the analogy. The teacher guides the children, having them focus on the parts they choose, how they behave, and how they feel. Comments such as the following might be generated:

> "I felt like I could take over."
>
> "I acted brave but was scared."
>
> "It was fun not being caged."

Following this experience, students discuss what they did, their motivations, and their feelings:

> "I thought the bigger animals might eat me."
>
> "I felt out of control."

Key words are often listed on the board and after most ideas are given, the group searches for contradictory statements such as "taking over" or feeling "out of control."

Step 5: Compressed Conflict

After finding all the contradictory pairs of words, the group chooses one. The teacher asks the students if they can think of something else that has these contradictory characteristics.

Step 6: Another Direct Analogy

For something combining the attributes "taking over" and "out of control," students might say a tornado, a drunk driver, a fire, and so on. These last direct analogies are examined to see how they relate to the compressed conflict inherent in taking over and being out of control.

Step 7: Reexamination of the Problem

At this point, the teacher returns to the playground situations. The students are asked to indicate how the experience has given them a better understanding of the playground problem or caused them to see it in a different way. They discuss their ideas and feelings and see if they can suggest a variety of ways to solve the playground hassle. They might say, for example, that the kids who are taking over are really out of control and that some control or direction should be provided for them. They might also be more sensitive to the feelings of power and fear the children have.

Step 8: Discuss the Synectics Process

The synectics process is discussed to see if the experience has enabled the students to better understand the problem on the playground.

Example 2—Characterization in Secondary Literature Class

Step 1: The Problem Presented

An understanding of central characters is critical to understanding literary works.

Step 2: The Problem Clarified

An understanding of Winston, a central character in George Orwell's *1984*, is essential to an understanding of the book.

Step 3: Direct Analogy

Students list animate and/or inanimate things that are like Winston:

> A reed that doesn't bend in the wind
>
> A broken toaster oven
>
> A test car

Step 4: Personal Analogy

Students choose one of the comparisons and using imagery, "become the thing." For example, they might become the test car. Students then process their experience, including acts, thoughts, or behaviors they experienced playing the analogy.

Step 5: Compressed Conflict

Contradictory words or phrases are chosen from the descriptions of experiences. For example, a test car may be described as very important and useless, as state of the art and out of date.

Step 6: Another Direct Analogy

Another direct analogy containing the contradictory terms is found. For example, for very important and useless, students might say monuments. For state of the art and out of date, they might give computers or news articles.

Step 7: Reexamination of the Problem

To conclude, the discussion returns to concentrate on Winston and to discuss how he is like the analogies.

Step 8: Discuss the Synectics Process

The synectics process is discussed to see if the experience has affected students' understanding of Winston.

Variations

Teachers can adapt synectics exercises to almost any content area or problem situation. Small groups could conduct their individual discussions and maintain their own lists as the teacher directs the overall process. The interplay between small group and large group discussion can be varied according to the grade level of the students.

Source: Adapted from Clasen, D. R., & Clasen, R. E. (1993) *Synectics in the classroom.* In P. J. Hillmann, D. R. Clasen, and R. E. Clasen (Eds.), *Teaching for thinking: Creativity in the classroom* (3rd ed.). Madison, WI: University of Wisconsin-Madison Educational Extension Programs. [Examples reproduced with permission.]

Daily Math Journal

Purpose

This strategy is useful to build two-way communication between teachers and students. By giving all students an opportunity to share their opinions and feelings regarding the learning of mathematics, the teacher can encourage persistence as students work to master the skills and knowledge in this sometimes confusing discipline.

TARGET Areas

Task; Recognition; Evaluation

Grade Level

This strategy can be adapted to almost all grade levels and content areas. It is especially useful in middle school.

Procedure

At the beginning of the semester, give students or ask them to purchase a small notebook that they can use as a daily journal. As an alternative, the teacher can fold several sheets of $8^1/2 \times 11$ paper together and staple them in the center. Each sheet will provide four pages for journal entries.

Students are asked to bring their math journals to class each day. At the end of each class, the teacher asks the students to spend a few minutes making an entry in their journal. A question or two can be listed on the chalkboard to help students focus their reactions. The following are examples of questions that teachers might use for this purpose:

1. What did you learn about mathematics today that you didn't know yesterday?
2. During our math lesson today, what confused you the most?
3. What can the teacher do to help you better learn math?
4. What do you like most about math class?
5. What do you like least about math class?
6. What are your opinions about the homework assisgnments in math class?
7. What do you think about the grade that you are earning in math class?

When first introducing daily mathematics journals, the teacher will find it useful to discuss the purpose of journal writing and the guidelines that students should keep in mind as they write. The teacher can emphasize that by knowing students' opinions and feelings about different aspects of the math class, he or she can better design assignments and exercises that help students overcome some of their difficulties with mastering math.

Emphasizing the following journal writing guidelines helps reduce student apprehension. It also can elicit information that will be useful for the teacher to encourage student persistence and to design or adjust learning activities that help students better understand and master math skills.

1. The thoughts and opinions that you write in your math journal are never right or wrong and they will not influence your grade in this class.
2. Please be as honest as you can.
3. Write as if you were talking to a friend.
4. If it is helpful, use diagrams to explain your thoughts.
5. If the question is difficult for you to answer, then write about why you are stuck.
6. Grammar and spelling will not be evaluated, but please write as clearly as you can.
7. Everything you write in your journal will be confidential.

Teachers will find it helpful to collect their students' journals about every two weeks. Although reading the journals and writing comments are time consuming, many teachers believe that the understanding and insights that they gain from the journals are well worth this extra effort.

Variations

Teachers can use daily journal writing in any subject area. Some teachers may choose to have students make weekly rather than daily entries. This change reduces the techer time required for reading and responding to student journals.

Some teachers find it useful to solicit anonymous student feedback regarding certain learning activities or the pace and clarity of instruction. Rather than as a substitute, anonymous evaluations are better used in addition to daily journals.

Source: Walter Siodlarz, middle school math teacher.

3.15

Fit My Category

Purpose

This strategy makes it possible for all students to experience success on a problem-solving task. It also supports group relatedness and belonging.

TARGET Areas

Task; Grouping; Evaluation

Grade Level

This strategy is especially appropriate for elementary and middle school, but can be adapted to some high school classes.

Procedure

This strategy is especially useful when you have an extra few minutes at the beginning or end of a class activity. Randomly select a student to begin the activity. Ask the student to think of a category in which to group students in the classroom. For example, the category could be those wearing jeans or tennis shoes, those with short hair, those with long sleeves, those wearing glasses, etc. The student does not reveal the category but calls on three students that fit the category to go to the front of the room.

The student who chose the category then goes around the room asking all class members if they think they fit the category or not. Each student answers "yes" or "no" depending on their observations and hypotheses regarding the category. If the students answer "yes," they join the group at the front of the room. If they answer "no," they remain in their seats. If students answer incorrectly, the student leader corrects them and they either join the group or stay in their seats.

When all students have made their guess, the group at the front of the room should include all those that fit the category. At this point, a student sitting at his or her desk can be called on to guess the category. If most students appear to have discovered the rule, those sitting at their desks can give the rule in unison. A student can then be randomly selected to be the leader the next time the game is played.

Variations

This activity can be adapted to high school language classes to help them work on vocabulary. Discovering and stating the category in a foreign language provides an added challenge.

Source: Adapted by Wendy Sallam, elementary school teacher.

3.16

Eliminating Failure

Purpose

This strategy is designed to overcome students' acceptance of unsatisfactory achievement and to increase their feelings of competence. It can also help reduce student anxiety related to tests.

TARGET Areas

Evaluation; Time

Grade Level

This strategy can be adapted to almost all grade levels and content areas in which unit tests are a primary factor in defining student success.

Procedure

This strategy requires that teachers have the authority to make a major change in their grading system. Some teachers may not have the autonomy to make the changes suggested in this strategy; administrative or board approval may be required.

When using this strategy, teachers may find it helpful to change their grading systems so that if students do not earn the grade of A, B, or C on unit tests, they can be given the grade of Incomplete rather than D or F.

If students receive an incomplete, they are allowed to continue with the class to the next unit, but are required to take a parallel retest covering the subject matter for which the incomplete was received. It becomes the student's responsibility for deciding the best strategy for remediating the unsatisfactory learning, but it is especially important that the teacher be willing to make time and to help in this process. The retest is evaluated with the same standard and grading system as the original test. This re-learning-retesting process continues until the student achieves a C- or higher.

If a student receives a second incomplete before a previous incomplete has been changed, the student is removed from the class and scheduled for independent study. This allows some students to slow down a bit if the pace of instruction is faster than they can handle; it allows others the time that they need to get caught up with the rest of the class. In practice, this instructional organization provides a remarkably effective procedure for underachieving students to experience success.

If administrative policies allow, it is most effective if students do not get credit for the course until all required units are completed with a grade of C- or higher. To support feelings of competence, it is important that students be allowed additional time to complete the required units in summer school or the following semester.

Clearly, this instructional approach requires more time and effort from teachers. Many of those that have tried it, however, believe that the increased student success makes it worth the effort.

Variations

To reduce scheduling difficulties, paid student tutors can be used in department offices or conference rooms to help students learn the outcomes being assessed. The student tutors might also be used to administer retests. Scheduling occasional enrichment activities for the class can create a breather for struggling students trying to catch up.

Source: Dennis Teichow, high school science teacher; Don Breen, high school English and social studies teacher.

Grading Rubrics

Purpose

This strategy can help all students experience a sense of competence from writing assignments.

TARGET Areas

Authority; Evaluation; Time

Grade Level

This strategy can be adapted to all grade levels and content areas that evaluate writing assignments.

Procedure

This strategy is based on the assumption that many students hand in poorly written or poorly thought-out assignments because they do not have a clear understanding of the teacher's expectations for a quality paper. To help students to improve the quality of their written assignments, teachers may find it useful to prepare and distribute a grading or evaluation rubric for each written assignment that students are required to complete.

Grading rubrics can take several forms, but often they simply define the teacher's expectations or evaluation criteria for earning an A, B, or C grade on a specific assignment. The more detailed and precise the grading rubric, the more helpful it will be in improving the quality of student performance. The following is an example of a generalized grading rubric that cn be adapted to specific writing assignments:

A paper—The student gives a complete analysis with a clear, coherent, and unambiguous explanation. The student demonstrates a thorough understanding of the important concepts or generalizations; provides rich, vivid, and powerful detail; and offers new insights into some aspects of the topic. Generalizations are supported with clear and appropriate examples.

B paper—The student gives a fairly complete description of the topic with reasonable explanations, although elements of the topic may lack detail and not be fully developed. Examples are used to support generalizations, although they may be briefly stated and limited.

C paper—The student minimally describes the topic, but the explanation may be muddled, incomplete, or vague. Examples are used to support some generalizations, but they may be inadequately described, demonstrate misconceptions, or be indirectly related to the generalizations.

Figure 3.4 provides a more detailed evaluation rubric for a self-study assignment used by the author in a course designed to help inservice and presevice teachers to increase student motivation to learn. The students receive a thorough description of the self-study assignment before the evaluation rubric is distributed.

Grading rubrics, by necessity, contain broad and encompassing statements like "thorough," "clear," "unambiguous," or "complete." To help students gain a clearer understanding of the teacher's definitions of these adjectives, it is often useful to save examples of previous A, B, and C papers to share with students. These can either be read and discussed with the class or examined by small groups of students.

Many teachers find it useful to allow students to rewrite papers that do not achieve the standard the student desires. Although this procedure requires significantly more time and effort from the teacher, it is a powerful strategy for improving student learning and feelings of competence.

Teachers will find the following books useful for establishing grading criteria and evaluation rubrics:

HERMAN, J., ASCHBACHER, P., & WINTERS, L. (1992). *A practical guide to alternative assessment.* Alexandria, VA: Association for Supervision and Curriculum Development.

FIGURE 3.4   Self-Study Evaluation Rubric

Grade of A—The student provides a detailed analysis of his or her professional aspirations and educational beliefs. A reflective assessment of personal strengths and weaknesses is provided and related to effectiveness as a teacher. From this description, it is clear that the student has considered several aspects of his or her role as a teacher and can see student motivation from several points of view. The student provides a clear description of the factors within the school environment that contribute to student apathy. A detailed description of the psychoacademic needs of students is presented, and the student identifies factors within the school environment that support or stifle these needs. The student presents structural changes and strategies, supported by examples, of how to help students meet each of these needs in the classroom. Finally, the student develops a statement of beliefs and personal philosophy for dealing with students that have given up on school learning.

Grade of B—The student provides an analysis of his or her professional aspirations, educational beliefs, and strengths and weaknesses as they relate to the teaching profession. Examples of positive and negative role models are provided. The discussion shows that the student can see academic apathy and noninvolvement from either the teacher or the student's point of view and provides a basic description of the factors that contribute to student apathy. The student demonstrates an understanding of some psychoacademic needs and identifies some factors that stifle these needs. The student presents one or two structural changes or strategies, partially supported by examples, to help students meet each of their psychoacademic needs in the classroom. Finally, the student develops a partial statement of beliefs and personal philosophy, either general in nature or inconsistent with previous statements, for dealing with students that have given up on school learning.

Grade of C—The student provides a vague or limited discussion of his or her professional aspirations and educational beliefs. When role models are presented, they are not related to the development of the student's educational beliefs. The discussion shows that the student is seeing student motivation from a limited point of view with little discussion of the factors that contribute to student apathy. Some suggestions or approaches for enhancing student motivation are provided, but they may be inconsistent with the student's educational belief statement or unrelated to the psychoacademic needs of students.

Self-Evaluation

Provide a one-page self-evaluation of your self-study based on the above scoring rubric. Include the specific grade that you think your paper should receive and include your reasons.

Marzano, R., Pickering, D., & McTighe, J. (1993). *Assessing student outcomes.* Alexandria, VA: Association for Supervision and Curriculum Development.

Wiggins, G. (1993). *Assessing student performance.* San Francisco: Jossey-Bass.

Variations

Rather than assigning letter grades, teachers may find it more effective to assign point values to elements of the grading rubric. These values can then be recorded and averaged to decide unit or quarter grades.

3.18

The "I Can" Can

Purpose

This strategy provides all students with a visual means to relish their successes and experience feelings of competence.

TARGET Areas

Task; Recognition; Evaluation

Grade Level

This strategy is most useful in primary and elementary grades.

Procedure

To help all students focus on their achievements and competencies, this strategy requires the teacher to ask each student to bring to class a clean metal can that has a plastic removable lid. A one-pound coffee can is ideal for this purpose, but any can will do. If the can does not have a plastic lid, a lid can be made from cardboard and taped to the top of the can. Next, students are asked to decorate the can with a strip of colorful paper taped to the can and decorated in some way that represents them, such as their favorite subject or sport. The paper strip should also include the label ' "I can" can.' The teacher uses sharp scissors to cut a two- or three-inch slot into the can lid. Depending on the nature of the classroom, students can keep their cans in their desks, along a back wall, in individual cubbies, or in any other convenient location designated by the teacher.

At the end of each day, students are asked to write on a small slip of paper one thing or one piece of information that they learned during the day that they are most proud of and that they could not do or did not know at the end of the previous day. They are asked to place the slip of paper into their "I can" can.

Approximately once a month, students are asked to open their "I can" cans and to read their slips of paper to themselves. The teacher then leads a class discussion of the new skills and information that students learned during the past month. They can discuss some of the skills that were most difficult to learn or took the most effort. They can also remember how it felt when they hadn't yet mastered the skill or information that they now have achieved.

By providing students with an opportunity to periodically examine their accomplishments and to recall their efforts, they can be encouraged to persist when they become frustrated with current learning.

Variations

Depending on the grade level of the students, the "I can" can can be opened more or less frequently. Students could also be encouraged to make a collage from their "I can" slips to decorate their classroom. This may be especially useful before parent-teacher conferences and open houses. Students can also be encouraged to empty their cans at the end of each quarter so their "I can" slips can be shared with parents.

Source: Adapted from Jones, V., & Jones, L. (1990). *Comprehensive Classroom Management* (3rd ed.). Boston: Allyn and Bacon.

3.19

The Death of "I Can't"

Purpose

This strategy is designed to build feelings of competence in students by helping them eliminate self-defeating thoughts and assertions.

TARGET Areas

Task; Authority

Grade Level

This strategy is particularly suited to upper elementary and middle school grades, but can be adapted to almost all levels and content areas.

Procedure

(This strategy requires some prearrangement and will probably need the endorsement of the school administration.) Write the statement "I can't . . . " on the chalkboard or on a transparency and ask each student to take out a clean sheet of theme paper. Next, ask the class to write out all the things that they can't do by completing the "I can't" statement as often as possible: statements like "I can't get a mountain bicycle," "I can't stand my brother," or "I can't understand fractions." Give the class several minutes to write down all the things they can't do. Additional sheets of paper should be available for those that need them.

When the group appears to be slowing, ask volunteers to read some of their items to the class. When most have had a chance to share their "I can't" statements, ask the class to use these ideas to continue to add to their lists. When most students have finished writing, ask them to put their lists in a small box on your desk. Close the box and tape it shut.

If you are doing this activity on a warm autumn day, instruct the class to leave everything on their desks, to be as quiet as possible, and to follow you. (The suspense of not knowing where they are going will pique their curiosity and interest.) Pick up the taped box and lead the group out of the classroom, into the hallway, and out the nearest exit. Keep the group moving to a remote area of the school property where you previously dug a small hole with a shovel brought from home or borrowed from the custodian. When the class arrives at the hole, ask them to form a circle. Place the box in the hole and then read a prepared eulogy similar to the following:

Gentlemen and ladies, we are gathered here this morning to bid farewell to a dear friend, someone whom we have grown to love and trust over the years, whose companionship we will miss dearly. It is with great sadness that we bid this farewell, for our lives will never be the same again. Yet, as sure as night follows day, our lives must go on and we must learn to live without our dear friend. Goodby, "I can't."

Next, pick up the shovel and put a little dirt on the box. Then pass the shovel around the group so that each student has a chance to participate in the burial. When the hole is covered, lead the group back to the classroom.

When everyone is back at their desks, take out a previously prepared posterboard tombstone decorated with: R. I. P. (rest in peace), "I can't" and tack it to a bulletin board near the front of the class. At this point, avoid discussing the burial or saying any more about the activity.

As the class continues with its regular schedule during the next few days, keep a sharp ear for any student saying "I can't" when confronted with a new assignment or task. Whenever you hear these self-defeating words from one of your students, all you need say is, "I'm sorry, he's not with us any more." It is at this point that students will begin to see the significance of their participation in the recent burial.

After students have realized that their good friend "I can't" is no longer allowed in the class, they will need help to learn to use the terms "I won't," "I don't," or "I choose not to" as a substitute. These terms reduce the sense of helplessness produced by "I can't" and help students develop a sense of ownership and personal responsibility for one's learning.

Variations

There are many ways to help eliminate "I can't" from students' normal vocabulary, but the mock funeral dramatizes the point. A trip to the school incinerator or garbage dumpster, however, may have the same effect. You might also encourage students to write their own eulogies that they can recite at the burial or cremation.

Source: Adapted from a presentation by Chick Moorman, educational consultant.

The One-Hour Book

Purpose

By providing students with the challenge of reading a novel in a brief period, this strategy builds feelings of competence in all students while promoting positive group interdependence.

TARGET Areas

Task; Grouping

Grade Level

This strategy is particularly useful for middle and high school levels and can be adapted to most content areas.

Procedure

Begin by selecting a novel that has about the same number of chapters as students in your class and is at a reading level that most of your students can handle. Try to select a book that will appeal to both boys and girls and does not have too many subplots or characters.

Explain to the class that they are going to read and discuss an entire novel during the next class period. To accomplish this task, it will be necessary for all students to contribute equally to this common goal. Show the book to the class and tell them the title and author. You may also want to briefly mention the setting for the story or any other information you believe is important to help them get started.

Next, ask each student to read a chapter of the book. This can be accomplished by cutting up a copy of the book and distributing chapters or by having enough copies for each student. Proficient readers can be given longer chapters and slower readers can be provided with shorter ones. If you have more students than chapters, cut up a second copy of the book so that some chapters will be read by two students.

Tell students that their task will be difficult because when they begin they will be confused by the identity of the characters and the sequence of events. Encourage them to persist in spite of this frustration and to do their best to derive meaning from the chapter. When all students have finished reading their chapters, ask them to give a two-minute presentation recounting the characters and events from their chapter. Inform students that they may take notes on a half sheet of paper, but discourage them from focusing on too many details.

The teacher should also read a chapter (preferably Chapter 1). This allows the teacher to model appropriate reading behavior and to reinforce the need for everyone to contribute to the goal of reading a novel in one hour.

When everyone is finished reading, the teacher begins the discussion by modeling the retelling of Chapter 1. The major characters and sequence of events are identified. Details that may relate to later incidents are also presented. It is important to strike a balance between too few and too many details and to stay within the two-minute time limit (this may be extended for those with longer chapters). Following the teacher's lead, students retell the book, chapter by chapter, until the story is complete.

As the students recall the significant events from their chapters, the following suggestions may be useful to help the teacher simplify the unfolding of the story:

1. Condense students' plot summaries into one or two sentences and write them on the chalkboard.
2. Ask open-ended questions of students who may be having difficulty supplying important information.
3. Remind students to retell their chapter rather than reread it to the group.
4. Supply important information that students may omit in their retelling (do this only if the information is crucial to understanding the plot or theme of the book).
5. When necessary, help tie subplots or fragmented actions together.

Variations

Depending on time constraints, the book could be read during a period of one day and discussed the following day. The retelling of the book can also be varied. The discussion of a middle chapter could precede an earlier chapter, especially if the book is long, to pique and hold interest during the retelling.

Source: Adapted from Lori Westra, middle school language arts teacher, and Cyrus Smith and Jan Hintz education professors.

CHAPTER FOUR

Strategies for Increasing Belonging and Relatedness

All human beings have a basic psychological need to relate to others in ways that reinforce their feelings of emotional security and belonging. They strive to establish contact, support, and a sense of community with others. These emotional bonds foster and maintain feelings of cohesion and contentedness, and it is through this relatedness that individuals come to know themselves as worthy and capable.

Cohesion, however, is not a natural or inevitable result of group activities. Its development requires an interdependence between group members and the employment of social interaction skills that support each member of the group.

RECOMMENDATIONS FOR BUILDING STUDENT RELATEDNESS

1. *Help students learn the skills of empathic listening.* Only by listening and accepting the feelings of others does one come to expect that one's own feelings will be heard and understood.

2. *Help students learn to express their feelings in ways that do not attack or injure others.* All individuals need to assume ownership of their feelings and to express them in ways that do not judge others.

3. *Take time to systematically help students learn to communicate acceptance and support for others.* Students need help in learning the skills of acceptance and interpersonal support.

4. *Help students learn and practice the skills of conflict resolution.* Students often turn to the teacher to "solve" their conflicts, rather than working to resolve them on their own. Yet students cannot be expected to settle conflicts without the prerequisite skill training.

5. *Attempt to develop group goals and positive interdependence in the classroom.* Cooperative learning activities can support intrinsic motivation by helping students identify and work toward common goals.

6. *Foster individual accountability for contributing to class and group goals.* Motivation is strengthened when students realize that their achievement and contributions are important to the success of others in the class.

7. *Avoid penalizing some students for the behavior of others.* Although group goals build positive interdependence, no one should be penalized for the behavior of others.

8. *Avoid forcing students to compete for a limited number of rewards.* Forced competition can contribute to detachment and alienation, and can undermine intrinsic motivation.

9. *Affirm the importance of affective goals within the classroom.* Affective goals support intrinsic motivation and should not be swept aside.

10. *Use feedback procedures to assess and discuss the interpersonal climate and personality of the classroom.* Intrinsic motivation is strengthened when students have an opportunity to assess how well they are doing in meeting their academic and interpersonal needs.

4.1

Cooperation Dilemma

Purpose

This strategy builds a sense of relatedness and autonomy by helping students learn the value of cooperation over competition in a simple game where cooperation rather than fighting yields a higher score for all participants.

TARGET Areas

Task; Authority; Recognition; Grouping; Evaluation; Time

Grade Level

This strategy is best suited for middle and high school.

Procedure

The teacher gives each student a packet of twenty-five small squares of scratch paper and a score sheet (see Figure 4.1), and asks students to sit back to back with a partner. The students write their name and their partner's name on the score sheet and are given the following instructions:

> *The object of this game is to earn as many points as you can. The game is played in twenty-five rounds. During a round, secretly write a C for co-*

FIGURE 4.1 Cooperate or Fight Score Sheet

	1	2	3	4	5	6	7	8	9	10	11	12	13	14	15	16	17	18	19	20	21	22	23	24	25
NAME:																									
PARTNER:																									

operate or an F for fight on one of your slips of paper. When finished, compare your answer with your partner's and score the round according to the following:

A. *Both players F = one point each*

B. *Both players C = three points each*

C. *One player F, one player C = player with F gets five points; player with C gets zero points*

Record your score, discard your used slips, and begin a new round when the teacher announces it. At the completion of your twenty-fifth round, total your score. Once the activity begins, you may not talk to your partner.

Since fighting yields a higher point value than cooperating, many students select this option more frequently in the early rounds. They reason that if their partner decides to cooperate, they will earn five points by fighting. The temptation to fight is strong even if their partner also decides to fight, since each will still receive one point.

The dilemma each player faces is that if both players fight, both do worse than if both had cooperated. Yet each may be reluctant to cooperate for fear that their partner will zap them with a fight and win five points. Some pairs quickly realize that if they cooperate all the time, they gain more points than those who are afraid to cooperate. However, if one student takes advantage of this trust, both partners will revert to fighting during the following rounds.

After all the points are totaled, the teacher may find it useful to lead a discussion on the game strategies that students chose, and how some pairs overcame the dilemma to cooperate rather than fight. The teacher might broaden this discussion to include historical confrontations and social interactions.

Variations

The teacher could begin this activity by making some pairs males, some females, and others mixed. The total scores of these subgroups could be compared and the results discussed in light of gender relationships. Some teachers may want to redesign this activity for use with groups of three or four students. This will require a similar scoring procedure that gives more points to fighting, but rewards group cooperation.

Source: Adapted from Philip Sanborn, high school history teacher.

Measuring the Motivational Climate

Purpose

This strategy builds a sense of group relatedness and autonomy by using student perceptions to provide the teacher with feedback regarding the motivational climate of the classroom.

TARGET Areas

Authority; Grouping; Evaluation

Grade Level

This strategy can be adapted to almost all grade levels and content areas.

Procedure

Duplicate the Motivational Climate inventory in Figure 4.2 or construct a similar inventory appropriate to the age and background of your students. Explain to the class that the purpose of answering the inventory is to help you better understand how class members view the content and learning activities and what changes or improvements you might make to increase their intrinsic motivation to learn.

Have the students complete the inventory anonymously, then compile the results by calculating a mean or average response for each item. You may find it useful to provide the class with a summary of these re-

FIGURE 4.2   Motivational Climate Inventory

Directions:

Please circle the number that best describes your opinion on each of the following items.

		Agree			Disagree	
1.	I understand most of the material covered in this class.	1	2	3	4	5
2.	Most of the time I try to do my best in this class.	1	2	3	4	5
3.	My classmates help one another learn.	1	2	3	4	5
4.	In this class I know how to ask for help when I need it.	1	2	3	4	5
5.	The teacher and the students in this class listen to each other.	1	2	3	4	5
6.	I usually find the assignments in this class interesting.	1	2	3	4	5
7.	What I learn in this class will help me learn other things.	1	2	3	4	5
8.	Most of what I learn in school will be of value to me.	1	2	3	4	5
9.	My teacher encourages me to do my best.	1	2	3	4	5
10.	I believe that I have choices in the way that I learn.	1	2	3	4	5
11.	I work hard for the grades that I receive.	1	2	3	4	5
12.	I believe that the grades that I receive are fair.	1	2	3	4	5
13.	My classroom is a friendly and safe place to learn.	1	2	3	4	5
14.	The students in my class care about each other.	1	2	3	4	5

sults and then conduct a discussion of intrinsic motivation and how it relates to the class. You might ask if the means of specific items surprise anyone or how the information can be used to meet both your academic objectives and the motivational interests of the class.

Utilizing student suggestions for making your learning activities more intrinsically motivating while still accomplishing your learning goal is a powerful way to build student autonomy and control over their learning. When the needs and opinions of both students and teachers are respected, learning thrives.

127

Appreciation Web

Purpose

This activity is designed to build a sense of group relatedness. It also encourages students to use positive statements in their relationships with others.

TARGET Areas

Recognition; Grouping

Grade Level

This strategy works best with elementary students, but can be adapted to middle school.

Procedure

Early in the year, the teacher asks the class to sit in a large circle. The teacher explains to the class that they are going to construct a web from a ball of yarn. (Depending on the background of the group, a discussion of webs might precede this activity.) The teacher starts by holding one end of the yarn and then throwing the yarn ball to a student across the circle. When the student catches the ball, the teacher makes a statement of appreciation regarding some behavior previously exhibited by the catcher.

For example, the teacher throws the yarn ball to Andrea, and after she catches it the teacher might say, "Andrea, I appreciate it when you take some of your recess time to clean the gerbil cage." Andrea says "Thank you" and then throws the yarn ball to another student followed by a statement of appreciation. This continues until all students have caught the yarn ball.

After the web is created, the teacher can lead a discussion of the symbolism represented by the web. The class might observe that they are all now connected and if one person lets go, the web unravels. They might also discuss how it feels to be appreciated by others and why it is sometimes difficult to express or receive appreciation. To remind the class of its sense of togetherness, the teacher could ask a colleague to take a photo of the finished web so that it can be displayed in the classroom.

Students unwind the web by reversing the process: The yarn ball is thrown back to the thrower, and as he or she winds the yarn, the receiver of the earlier appreciation statement now makes a statement of appreciation to the thrower, who continues the process until the ball is finally thrown back to the teacher.

Variations

Put-ups, similar to those identified in Strategy 2.3, could be substituted for statements of appreciation.

Source: Adapted from Maureen Lucey, elementary school teacher.

Brainstorming Bonanza

Purpose

This strategy fosters relatedness and competence by enabling all students to contribute to a common goal. It can also be used as an icebreaking activity for cooperative learning groups.

TARGET Areas

Task; Grouping; Evaluation

Grade Level

By varying the topics, this strategy can be adapted to almost all grade levels and content areas.

Procedure

The teacher divides the class into groups of four or five students. This can be accomplished by assigning students to specific groups, by using the random grouping procedure discussed in strategy 4.6, or by allowing students to choose their groups. This strategy is particularly useful as an icebreaking activity for cooperative learning groups that will stay together for other learning tasks.

The teacher gives each group two pencils and two pads of paper and asks group members to decide who will record answers and who will serve as the group's spokesperson. These roles can be shared.

The teacher begins the activity by giving the students a general category or one related specifically to the course content. The teacher then allows students one minute to write down as many responses as they can for the topic. For example, the category could be "Things that fly" or "Countries in Africa."

When the minute is up, students are asked to put their pencils down. The teacher writes each group's name or number on the chalkboard and then asks the first group for an answer. If the answer meets the requirements of the category and has not been previously given, the teacher gives the group one point. The teacher then asks the second group for an answer, and so on. Each group is allowed to give only one answer at a time, and an answer can only be used once. A group loses its turn if it offers an answer that has previously been mentioned. This encourages students to be organized and to listen to the responses of others.

The first round is completed when each group is given a chance to respond. The second round begins with group two, rather than group one, the third round with group three, and so on. When a group has exhausted their answers, they must pass for each subsequent round until all groups have finished. The points can then be counted and the winning team congratulated. A new category can then be selected.

Possible categories could include the following:

Famous authors; things that float; types of cars; holidays; bodies of water; worst Christmas gifts; things you see in the impulse buying aisle; things you read, places to put a comma; parts of a frog; names of computer programs; types of trees; vegetables; fruits; cuts of beef; prime numbers; Civil War battles; states that border the Atlantic Ocean; NFL football teams; orchestra instruments; and so on.

Source: Amy Christianson, elementary school librarian.

4.5

Nuts and Bolts

Purpose

This strategy is designed to build group cohesiveness, relatedness, and interdependence.

TARGET Areas

Task; Grouping

Grade Level

This strategy is most effective in middle school, but it can be adapted to almost all grade levels.

Procedure

Divide the class into groups of four to six students. Give each group a packet of material and ask students not to open the packet until instructed. Next, explain that each packet contains bolts, washers, and nuts in three different sizes (see materials list). The task of each team is to work as quickly as possible to assemble the nuts and washers onto the bolts in the following order (using Figure 4.3, write this information on the chalkboard):

FIGURE 4.3 Nuts and Bolts

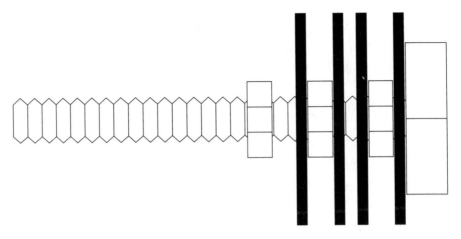

1. Washer
2. Nut
3. Washer
4. Washer
5. Nut
6. Washer
7. Nut

The teacher should tighten all nuts snugly to the bolt and use a stopwatch to determine the number of seconds that each group takes to complete the task. After the instructions are understood and the stopwatch readied, the teacher should tell the groups to begin.

Usually, there is considerable variance in the time that each group takes to complete the task. After the first trial, the bolts should be disassembled and all hardware placed back into the bag. The groups should then discuss how they went about assembling their bolts and what changes they could make to improve the efficiency. The groups are then given a second chance competing against the stopwatch to complete the task.

After the second trial, the class should be encouraged to discuss how each group partitioned the labor needed to complete the task. The discussion will likely focus on the importance of teamwork and of having each member contribute to the final outcome. A third or fourth trial could be used to determine which students were most efficient at each of the tasks.

Variations

The amount of hardware provided and the sizes of the groups can be adjusted to the grade level and manual dexterity of the class. Team competition might be used, but the focus of the activity should be on how teamwork and shared responsibility can improve the group's efficiency.

Materials

One bag of hardware for each group containing the following:

(1) $1/4$ inch bolt approximately 1 inch long

(1) $5/16$ inch bolt approximately $1^1/4$ inches long

(1) $3/8$ inch bolt approximately $1^1/2$ inches long

(3) $1/4$ inch nuts

(3) $5/16$ inch nuts

(3) $3/8$ inch nuts

(4) $1/4$ inch washers

(4) $5/16$ inch washers

(4) $3/8$ inch washers

Source: Suggested by Ron Sdano, middle school health teacher.

Random Grouping

Purpose

This strategy can be used to build a sense of group relatedness. It provides teachers with an interesting and efficient method for randomly grouping and regrouping students.

TARGET Areas

Authority; Grouping

Grade Level

This strategy can be adapted to all grade levels, although elementary and middle school students seem to especially enjoy using it.

Procedure

This strategy requires that the teacher provide each student in the class with a slip of construction paper that varies in size, shape, color, and marking. The teacher can tape these slips inside student desks, notebooks, or textbooks for use throughout the semester. Depending on the size of the groups required, the teacher or a student can randomly choose one of several combinations to form the groups. Teachers can use the following directions for preparing slips for up to thirty-two students (the task is not as complicated as it appears):

135

Directions

1. Start with two piles of sixteen four-inch squares of paper. Each pile should be a different color (red and blue will be used in this example).
2. Divide each pile in half. Take one of the red piles and cut each square into a triangle. Do the same to one of the blue piles.
3. Regroup the slips into the following new piles:

   Eight red triangles

   Eight blue triangles

   Eight red squares

   Eight blue squares

4. Divide each of these four piles in half. Take a red triangle pile and cut each triangle into a smaller triangle (see Figure 4.4). Do the same with a pile of the blue triangles.
5. Take one of the red square piles and cut each square into a smaller square (see Figure 4.4). Do the same with a pile of the blue squares.
6. Regroup the slips into the following new piles:

   Four small red triangles

   Four large red triangles

   Four small blue triangles

   Four large blue triangles

   Four small red squares

   Four large red squares

   Four small blue squares

   Four large blue squares

7. Divide each of these eight piles in half. Take a small red triangle pile and with a marker, make one dot in the middle of each triangle (see Figure 4.4). Do the same with a pile of large red triangles, small blue triangles, large blue triangles, small red squares, large red squares, small blue squares, and large blue squares (see Figure 4.4).
8. Using the marker, make two dots in the middle of each of the remaining sixteen slips of paper.

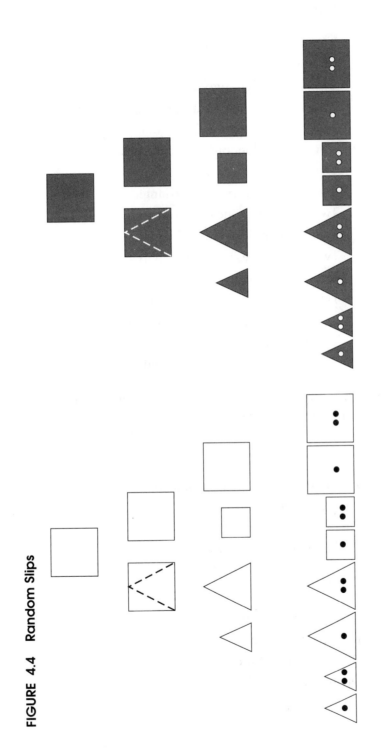

FIGURE 4.4   Random Slips

137

9. If all went well, you should have the following sixteen piles of slips:

Two small, red, one dot, squares
Two small, red, one dot, triangles
Two small, blue, two dot, squares
Two small, blue, two dot, triangles
Two small, blue, one dot, squares
Two small, blue, one dot, triangles
Two small, blue, two dot, squares
Two small, red, two dot, triangles
Two large, red, one dot, squares
Two large, red, one dot, triangles
Two large, blue, two dot, squares
Two large, blue, two dot, triangles
Two large, blue, one dot, squares
Two large, blue, one dot, triangles
Two large, blue, two dot, squares
Two large, red, two dot, triangles

Place slips in a box, shake them, and distribute them to students as they enter the class for the first time. The teacher now has the following options for dividing the class into groups:

To form *two* groups of *sixteen*:

Divide by shape (square/triangle)
Divide by size (large/small)
Divide by color (red/blue)
Divide by dots (one/two)

To form *four* groups of *eight*:

Divide by shape and size
Divide by shape and color
Divide by shape and dots
Divide by size and color
Divide by size and dots

Divide by color and dots

To form *eight* groups of *four*:

Divide by shape, size, and color
Divide by shape, size, and dots
Divide by size, color, and dots

To form *sixteen* groups of *two*:

Divide by shape, size, color, and dots

Variations

Adding a fifth category, such as drawing a circle around half of the dots, will allow for up to sixty-four students. A sixth category will double the number again.

Some teachers may find it useful to laminate the slips so that they can use them over again with different classes. (It will be easier to start with laminated paper rather than to laminate each individual piece.) The laminated slips can then be kept in a box, and on days when grouping is required, students can draw a slip from the box as they enter the classroom.

By using a separate three by five card to write each of the various combinations to make groups of sixteen, eight, and four students (only one combination is possible for partners), the teacher or an assigned student can draw the grouping combination procedure for any given activity. This will allow for additional random variation in grouping, and will enable students to work with more class members.

When the class is composed of fewer than thirty-two students, the teacher should remove slips in pairs, starting with one-dot/two-dot slips, followed by one-dot/two-dot large and one-dot/two-dot small, and so on. With an odd number of students in the room, one group of two will have three students; when groups of four are being formed, one, two, or three groups of four will have five students. (When possible, the group of three students might also be used.)

Icebreakers

Purpose

Icebreakers are useful for building a sense of belonging during the first weeks of school or when students in a classroom are strangers to one another.

TARGET Areas

Task; Recognition; Grouping

Grade Level

This strategy can be adapted to almost all grade levels and content areas.

Procedure

Rhyming Names

Students should sit in a circle for this activity. One student begins by giving his or her first name preceded by an adjective that describes him (Jovial Jim, for example). The student to the left of the starter then repeats that name and adjective and adds her own name and adjective (Jovial Jim, and I'm Silly Sally). This continues until everyone in the class has repeated the names and adjectives and added their own (Jovial Jim,

Silly Sally, Tired Tom, Lovable Lora, Perceptive Pam, etc.). The teacher should instruct students not to write names down, but if they have difficulty remembering a particular student's name as they go around the circle, that student can mention the adjective as a clue.

The Minute Monologue

The teacher writes plural nouns on slips of paper (a minimum of one slip per student) and places them in a hat or box. (Examples: cows, chickens, airplanes, cookies, cars, snowflakes, etc.) A student who has a watch with a second hand or digital seconds is appointed timekeeper. The hat is passed to the first student and he or she selects a slip of paper. That student is required to make up a story about him or herself and the plural noun and speak for sixty seconds.

Treasured Object

The teacher proposes the following hypothetical question to the class, "If your home was on fire and you were only able to save one item from your room, what would you select and why would you select it?" Going around the circle, each student is given time to explain his or her choice and the reason that item was selected over others.

Birthday Circle

Students stand in the center of the room and are told that their task is to place themselves into a chronological circle according to the month and date of their birthday. They are told that they cannot speak during this exercise, but that they can use their fingers to communicate their month and date.

After everyone is standing where they think they should be located, students take a turn saying their birthday and adjusting their position.

Big and Little Buddies

Purpose

This strategy reinforces a sense of relatedness and autonomy for both primary and upper elementary school students.

TARGET Areas

Task; Authority; Recognition; Grouping

Grade Level

This strategy is designed for primary and upper elementary school students.

Procedure

By matching students in primary classes with students in upper elementary classes, teachers can create learning partnerships that benefit students at both levels. Kindergarten teachers, for example, could collaborate with fourth grade teachers to create student partnerships. Similarly, first grade classes could work with fifth grade classes, and second grade classes with sixth grade classes. Other combinations are possible, however, depending on the grade levels of the teachers that choose to participate. Once classes have decided to work together, the two teachers can decide the student matches. Or teachers can enhance the autonomy of upper grade students by allowing them to choose their little buddies from the primary class list.

With kindergarten classes, the teacher can start the activity by reading the kindergartners an interesting story. After the story, the students are given a large sheet of paper and are instructed to fold the paper in half. The teacher then asks the students to use the left side of their paper to draw a picture that tells a story about themselves and the characters from the story. Next, the big and little buddies are matched, and the teachers assign half of the pairs to each classroom.

The kindergartners describe their stories to their big buddies, and the big buddies write out the story on the right side of the paper. When they have finished, the big buddy reads the story to his or her little buddy. Later, when the students have returned to their original classrooms, the kindergartners read their story to the teacher or to each other in small groups.

Similar activities can be used with first and second grade classes. For example, rather than drawing a story from a book, the primary grade students could draw stories that describe their experiences on Thanksgiving or Christmas Day and the big buddy transcribes the story when they are finished.

Variations

Big and little buddies can be organized for activities other than reading and writing. They can be useful for helping primary grade students practice basic math or spelling skills, or for giving older students opportunities to display artistic, scientific, or geographical skills and information.

Source: Suggested by Jane Westmas and Linda Santy elementary school teachers.

Tropical Tribune

Purpose

This strategy builds a strong sense of group relatedness, autonomy, and competence through the creation of a class newspaper. This example shows how a small class project evolved into a nationally distributed publication.

TARGET Areas

Task; Authority; Recognition; Grouping

Grade Level

This strategy can be adapted to almost all grade levels and content areas.

Procedure

Teachers will find the creation of a class newspaper to be a productive culminating project for almost any unit of study. In this example, several classes of sixth grade students participated in an extensive unit about tropical rainforests (see Figure 4.5).

Teachers asked students to choose one of the following four groups in which to work: entertainment, editorial, news, and features. Each work group was composed of two student editors, a teacher, and parent and

FIGURE 4.5 Background Information about the Tropical Tribune

The students at J.C. McKenna Middle School have been studying tropical rainforests since 1988. They were among the first group of students in the State of Wisconsin to purchase rainforest acres and to protect them for future generations. Teachers and students at the school create an annual newspaper that includes student articles about rainforests and other environmental issues. The paper is called the *Tropical Tribune* and is made available for national distribution. It is known for providing accurate and reliable information about the problems of rainforests and how others can help the situation by networking student projects and interests.

The *Tropical Tribune* is the only student-written rainforest publication in the United States. Sixteen hundred copies of the first two issues have been distributed to individuals in forty-three states, Canada, Australia, and Costa Rica, and the number of orders continues to expand.

Readers of the *Tropical Tribune* have been made more aware of the circumstances surrounding rainforests and many have used ideas from the students' newspaper for class projects, to purchase and preserve rainforest acreage, and to contact their congresspersons. The newspaper helps foster environmental awareness on a global level, and it invites students to become active participants in the ecological problems of rainforests.

The project's success has been beyond expectations. The work of the students has been recognized by U.S. Senators and Representatives, zoo directors, state superintendents of schools, and university professors. The Earth Foundation, Save the Rainforest, Inc., Rainforest Action Network, and Ecosystem Survival Plan have all encouraged and supported the *Tropical Tribune*. Save the Rainforest, Inc. has asked the McKenna students to use the *Tropical Tribune* to help answer all of the student mail that they receive. Dr. Daniel Janzen, Professor of Biology at the University of Pennsylvania and Director of Instituto Nacional de Biodiversidad (INBio), has asked the newspaper to help spread the word to students throughout the United States about how they can assist in his projects in Costa Rica.

According to teachers at McKenna Middle School, the paper is based on the premise that when students learn about social and environmental problems, they need some recourse to act on their new knowledge. Networking students with a student created paper empowers them. They learn that they are not helpless or without hope—they can make a difference. The *Tropical Tribune* is J.C. McKenna Middle School's contribution to this effort.

Subscriptions can be obtained by sending $3.00 to:

Tropical Tribune
J.C. McKenna Middle School
307 S. First St.
Evansville, WI 53536

community volunteers. One of the sixth grade classrooms was used to house research materials.

Throughout the project, teachers tried to help students integrate newspaper skills with their language arts and reading curriculum. As the students learned about rainforests, they kept a list of potential story ideas on the bulletin board. Students also took field trips to a local newspaper and to a historical society rainforest exhibition.

As the unit progressed, groups brainstormed story ideas. Then, in collaboration with their editors, topics were assigned. Students who had difficulty writing were teamed with more skilled writers or could choose to work on art and graphic layouts.

An entire school day was devoted to the rainforest project. Other classes were canceled, and students spent the day listening to talks by rainforest experts and environmental leaders, writing, editing, and entering stories into the class computers. Students interviewed the volunteer consultants to gain material for articles to be included in the newspaper.

As the stories were completed, student editors, with the help of teachers, decided what stories would be included. They also returned stories that could be improved by rewriting. The editors took responsibility for finances, layout of the paper, and other details of the production. Issues like the title and logo design were voted on by the entire class.

At the end of the unit, the final product was duplicated and distributed. The original newspaper was so well received that it was eventually sent to a diverse group of people and organizations, and was marketed through environmental periodicals and teacher publications. Throughout the project, students were encouraged to make their own decisions about content and distribution.

Students at J.C. McKenna Middle School, Evansville, WI work on the next issue of the Tropical Tribune

Later in the year a second issue of the paper was created so that more students could have their work published. The two issues are now recreated each year by the incoming sixth grade.

Variations

The variations on the theme and procedure are endless. The key is to ensure that students believe that they are providing a worthwhile service and that they envision the product as theirs and not their teacher's.

Source: Harold Beedle, middle school social studies teacher.

Five Squares

Purpose

This strategy builds group cooperation and relatedness by requiring each individual to contribute toward reaching a group goal.

TARGET Areas

Task; Grouping; Evaluation

Grade Level

This strategy is particularly useful at middle and high school levels.

Procedure

This strategy requires about one hour of preparation time to construct the puzzle sets (see Figure 4.6). To begin the activity, divide the class into groups of five. If one or two students remain after this division, they can be asked to collaborate with a member in one of the groups. If three of four students remain, they can form their own smaller group.

Each group is given a puzzle set consisting of five envelopes with one envelope going to each group member. Students are told that at the teacher's signal they are to use the puzzle pieces in the envelopes to construct a six-inch square. Puzzle pieces are passed among the group mem-

FIGURE 4.6 Five Squares

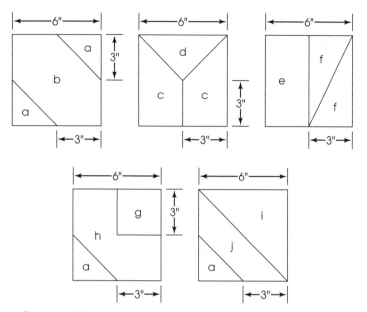

Instructions: Draw the following patterns on five pieces of stiff paper. One set of five patterns is needed for each group of five students. Lightly pencil the letters a through j as shown above and cut each square into the designated pieces. Clearly mark five envelopes A through E and distribute the pieces thus:

Envelope A—j, h, e
Envelope B—a, a, a, c
Envelope C—a, j
Envelope D—d, f
Envelope E—g, b, f, c

Finally, erase the lowercase letters and write the corresponding envelope letters on each piece so that they can be returned to their envelopes for reuse.

Source: Adapted with permission from Jones, V. & Jones, S. (1986). *Comprehensive class-room management* (3rd ed.). Boston: Allyn & Bacon, Inc., p. 117.

bers until the five equally sized squares are constructed. The following three rules are to be followed by all participants:

1. No member may speak until all the squares are completed
2. No member may signal in any way that he or she wants a particular piece
3. Individuals may offer pieces to others

Groups that complete their task can be allowed to quietly observe other groups at work. Depending on the age of the students, if group members have difficulty completing the task, they can raise their hand to signal the teacher to replace them with a student from a group that has finished.

When all groups have completed the task, the teacher can lead a discussion on the behaviors that facilitated task completion and those that hindered the process. Remind students to avoid mentioning names as they describe behaviors that blocked or helped.

Variations

The envelope sets could be reconfigured for groups of less than five.

Source: Adapted with permission from Jones, V., & Jones, L. (1990). *Comprehensive classroom management* (3rd ed.). Boston: Allyn and Bacon, Inc. p. 117, reproduced by permission of the publisher.

4.11

Assertive, Aggressive, or Passive?

Purpose

This strategy supports students' feelings of relatedness and autonomy by helping them communicate more effectively with others.

TARGET Areas

Authority; Grouping

Grade Level

This strategy is most useful in middle and high school.

Procedure

This strategy helps student distinguish between aggressive, assertive, and passive behavior and communication styles. Teachers should start this activity by explaining the differences between these three styles. They might point out that people communicating aggressively usually state their feelings clearly, but often put others down or elicit a defensive or negative response as they try to satisfy their needs. People communicating passively usually give in to avoid a conflict and are often reluctant to express how they really feel. Assertive communication, however, is usually honest and direct, but not injurious to others. The following example might help students recognize these differences:

After school a friend asks you to take several books back to the library, but you would rather not.

Aggressive response: No way. You are always asking me to do things for you just because you are too lazy.

Passive response: Oh, all right. I have other things to do, but I guess I can find time to do it.

Assertive response: No, I'd rather not do that. I have other things that I would like to do right now.

After discussing the differences between these three response styles, the teacher hands out the list of ten situations in Figure 4.7 and asks students to rate each of the response alternatives using a plus (+) for an aggressive response, zero (0) for an assertive response, and a minus (–) for a passive response. The class is then divided into small groups to discuss their answers and to arrive at a group rating for each item. The class can discuss any discrepancies between individual ratings and group ratings. Students might also want to discuss how they would feel in each situation.

Variations

The class could role play each situation with different students playing aggressive, passive, or assertive roles. They might also want to dramatize how they feel when being the recipients of these three response styles.

Source: Adapted by Jerry Basler, high school teacher.

FIGURE 4.7   Assertive, Aggressive, or Passive

Situation 1

You have a lot of homework and your mother asks you to do the dishes.

Response

Why don't you do the dishes? Can't you see I have tons of homework?

All right, Mom.

I have a ton of homework tonight, and I'd rather not have to do the dishes so I can get my work finished.

Situation 2

Several friends at a party ask you to try drugs, but you don't want to do it.

FIGURE 4.7 *Continued*

Response

    Well, just this once won't hurt.

    You're all crazy! What do you want to do that for?

    No thanks, I really don't want to try drugs.

Situation 3

Your teacher has made a mistake grading your exam.

Response

    You cheated me out of ten points on this problem.

    I've discovered an error in the way my test was corrected.

    Do nothing.

Situation 4

Your girlfriend knows your parents will be out of town and wants to have a party at your house. You do not want to break your promise to your parents not to have a bunch of people over, but you don't want to make your girlfriend angry at you. You are not busy that night.

Response

    My cousin's coming from out of town and I have to be with him.

    How can you think of doing something like that? What would happen if anyone found out?

    I don't feel right about doing that. Let's go to a movie instead.

Situation 5

Your friend wants to copy your homework and you believe that copying is wrong.

Response

    I worked hard on this and I want the full credit for the assignment. I don't want to take the chance of getting caught.

    Well, OK. Be sure to change the words some.

    That's cheating.

Situation 6

You would like to be nominated for student council.

Response

    I think I am qualified and would like to be nominated for student council.

    Don't nominate Mark; he's a creep.

Continued

FIGURE 4.7 *Continued*

You think to yourself, I hope someone nominates me.

Situation 7

Someone you do not want to go out with asks you to a dance. She is the first to ask you.

Response

I'm sorry, I already have a date.

What? Sorry, I'm busy.

Thanks for asking, but I'd rather not.

Situation 8

Your parents want you to attend the college they went to, but you would rather go somewhere else.

Response

I'll think about what you have said, but I need to make my own decision.

You always try to run my life. Get off my back!

If you're sure that's what is best.

Situation 9

You are talking to your girlfriend and suddenly realize that if you don't leave immediately you will be late for work. She wants to keep talking.

Response

I really ought to be going.

Oh, no, you don't! You're making me late for work.

I know you want to talk more and we'll get together after I'm through working. See you.

Situation 10

You want to enroll in home economics but people are trying to discourage you by calling you names and making fun of you. They do not think being good at household tasks is very important for a man.

Response

Get lost. I'll do as I please.

I want to learn to be a chef. You'll probably be surprised some day at what I can do.

Not enroll in the class.

From *Challenges: A Young Man's Journal for Self-awareness and Personal Planning,* by M. Bingham, J. Edmondson, & S. Stryker, 1994. Copyright Girls Incorporated of Greater Santa Barbara. Reprinted with permission of Advocacy Press, P.O. Box 236, Santa Barbara, CA 93102. Not to be duplicated in any other form.

154

Gumdrop Tower

Purpose

This strategy helps build a sense of group relatedness by allowing students to discover how different styles of leadership can affect group satisfaction and performance.

TARGET Areas

Task; Authority; Recognition; Grouping; Evaluation

Grade Level

This strategy is useful for upper elementary, middle, and high school students

Procedure

This activity provides students with an opportunity to experience and compare the results of autocratic, democratic, and laissez-faire styles of leadership. The class is told that they are going to construct gumdrop towers. The teacher divides the class into six groups and assigns each group a number from one to six. Students select one member within each group to serve as the group leader. As the groups are forming their circles (they may want to use the floor or large tables for this activity), the teacher meets with the six group leaders in a corner of the room. The teacher gives each leader either a democratic, autocratic, or laissez-faire instruction card (see below). They are asked to read the instructions carefully and not to show their cards to anyone. Before beginning the activity the teacher should type the following instructions for each leadership style on three by five cards, making a total of six cards with two sets of instructions for each leadership style:

Democratic—Your task is to demonstrate democratic leadership without letting your group know what you are doing. You should try to encourage everyone to get involved in the project. When suggestions are made, you should try to make sure that everyone agrees before the group does it. As a democratic leader, you will want to make sure that all your group members believe that they had an equal say in the construction of your tower.

Autocratic—Your task is to act like a friendly dictator during the construction project without letting your group know what you are doing. While others may offer suggestions, you should try to make sure that only your ideas are the ones that are used. Give orders to others about what they should do during the construction. Without overdoing it, take control of the project and construct the tower from your ideas.

Laissez-faire—Your task is to demonstrate a hands-off style of leadership without letting your group know what you are doing. Let everyone in your group do what he or she wants, and don't offer any ideas or suggestions on how the tower should be constructed.

After the leaders understand their instructions, they should put their cards away and return to their groups. The teacher than announces to the class that the task of each group is to construct the best tower that they can from the materials they are given. They will have about thirty minutes to complete their structures, at which time the principal (vice principal, secretary, janitor, etc.) will be asked to judge the towers according to height, strength, and originality, with equal weight being given to each category.

Give each group one large bag of gumdrops, a box of round toothpicks, and a box of twenty drinking straws with which to complete their towers. Encourage class members to avoid eating the gumdrops until the project is finished.

After thirty minutes, ask each group to bring their tower to the front of the room and then return to their seats and complete the following questionnaire:

Group Number

On a scale of 1 to 5 (1 being low and 5 high), please rate the following:

_____ 1. Satisfaction with your group leader

_____ 2. Satisfaction with your group's tower

_____ 3. Satisfaction with your contributions to the tower

While students are completing the questionnaire, put a copy of Table 4.1 on the chalkboard and ask the judge or judges to complete the first part of the table by rating each tower on a scale of 1 to 5 (1 being low and 5 high).

Ask volunteers to collect the student questionnaires and to calculate the average on the three statements for each group. They can then enter these scores in the second part of the table.

The teacher next asks the group leaders to read their leadership instructions while the teacher writes the corresponding style in the third part of the table.

After the table is completed, the teacher leads a discussion of the activity using the following questions as a guide:

1. Do you see any relationship between leadership style and the judge's ratings?
2. How are individual contributions related to the judge's ratings?
3. Is there a relationship between leadership style and individual contributions? What leadership style produced the greatest participation? Which style produced the least?
4. How is individual satisfaction with the group product related to the judge's ratings?
5. What relationships do you see between satisfaction with the group leader and the style of leadership?
6. What other conclusions regarding group cooperation, productivity, and leadership have you learned from this activity?

Variations

The teacher may choose to offer a prize to the tower with the highest rating. If this is done, it is important to discuss how this competitive dimension influenced student participation or the quality of the group products.

TABLE 4.1 Gumdrop Tower Evaluation

| GROUP | External Evaluation | | | | Group's Satisfaction | | | LEADERSHIP STYLE |
	HEIGHT	STRENGTH	ORIGINALITY	LEADER	TOWER	CONTRIBUTION	
1							
2							
3							
4							
5							
6							

Based on the age of the group, additional or substitute construction materials may be used.

Source: Adapted from Jane Conover, high school art teacher; Pfeiffer & Jones (1974).

Group Filmstrips

Purpose

This strategy builds group cooperation and relatedness while encouraging creativity in a reading enrichment activity.

TARGET Areas

Task; Authority; Recognition; Grouping

Grade Level

This strategy can be adapted to almost all grade levels and content areas.

Procedure

Divide the class into groups of four to six students. Inform the groups that this activity will give them an opportunity to write and produce their own creative filmstrip story. Begin by inviting each group to elect a recorder and to brainstorm story activities. Encourage them to discuss each idea carefully and then to vote on one idea that their group will use. As they discuss their story idea they will be required to make decisions about the story title, setting, number of characters, plot, and sequence of events.

Once the groups have agreed on the story outline, encourage them to divide the following work tasks:

1. Photographer (should have access to an inexpensive 35 mm camera)
2. Narrator (should have access to an inexpensive cassette tape recorder)
3. Artists (should enjoy drawing; two or three will be needed)
4. Titlists (should have good printing)
5. Characters (should work with the narrator to record appropriate dialogue)

The teacher should make an ample supply of 24" by 36" white construction paper and colored felt markers available to the artists and titlists of each group. Once the groups have developed their story ideas, they should decide the number, composition, and sequence of the pictures and titles that will be required to tell their story. They may want to use a sheet of construction paper with printed titles, hand-drawn illustrations, or pictures from magazines for each frame. Since 35 mm color slide film usually comes in 24 exposure rolls, each group should limit their filmstrip to 24 frames.

The photographer should be in charge of photographing the construction paper pictures, and should take all shots horizontally. It is important that whoever takes the film for processing give instructions that the processed slide film should not be mounted or cut.

The narrator is responsible for making the audiotape sequenced to the filmstrip. He or she will likely read parts of the story and then record appropriate dialogue among the story characters that correspond to each picture. A bell or clicker can be used to instruct the projectionist to advance frames.

At the completion of the activity, each group can show its filmstrip to the class. Group members might also take turns taking the filmstrip home to share with parents and friends.

The cost for construction paper, film, and processing will be expensive, so teachers should be creative in finding funding sources for this activity. Often student or parent/teacher organizations will donate money or materials and supply accounts might be used.

Variations

The first time that this strategy is introduced, younger students might find it difficult to create their own stories. Here it may be easier for them to copy parts of a book or to use a familiar story to make their filmstrip. Special events or holidays might also be sued to generate story ideas.

If the budget is limited, large groups or a class filmstrip can save on expenses.

Source: Suggested by Julie Brandt, elementary school teacher.

4.14

Pinwheels

Purpose

This strategy provides a structural activity that supports group relatedness by using the efforts of all class members to help each student master content objectives. It builds positive interdependence and individual accountability while fostering a sense of belonging and relatedness each participant.

TARGET Areas

Task; Grouping

Grade Level

This strategy can be adapted to almost all grade levels and content areas.

Procedure

Divide the class into an even number of groups of three, four, or five students. If there are an odd number of students in the class, the teacher can join a group to make an even number. To set up the pinwheels, have one group (assuming four students per group) come to the front of the class and stand back to back, each facing a different direction: north, south, east, and west. Ask the students to stand so that their shoulders are barely touching. Ask a second group of four to form a circle around the first group, each facing a member of the first group (see Figure 4.8). Form additional pinwheels following the same procedure. Some pinwheels may have to consist of two, three, or five students to ensure that all students have an opportunity to participate.

To use this procedure with spelling, for example, give each student a 3 by 5 card with three or four words taken from the weekly list. It doesn't matter if several words are repeated, just as long as all the words are included at least once in each pinwheel.

To being the pinwheel action, inside students read the first word on their lists to their outside partners, who are asked to spell the word correctly. The person reading the word corrects any errors in their partner's spelling and tries to offer a mnemonic device or strategy for spelling the word correctly, e.g., "i before e, except after c." When the inside students have finished helping their outside partner spell their words, the outside students repeat the process using their list of words with the inside students.

FIGURE 4.8 Pinwheels

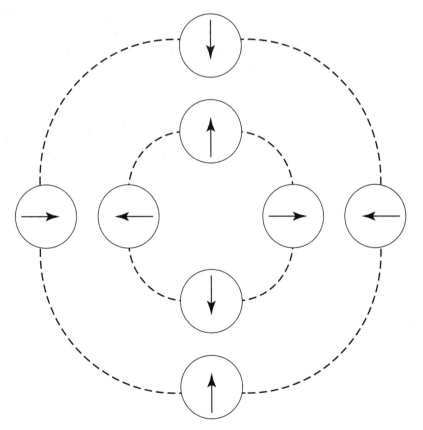

When the first round is finished, the teacher gives the signal for the outside ring of students to spin one student to their left. Each student is now facing a new partner, and the sequence of reviewing and learning the spelling words is repeated. When they have finished, the outside ring of students again spins one student to the left and repeats the process. After the pinwheel circuit is completed and students are standing in front of their original partner, students in the inside circle are asked to exchange cards with their partner in the outside circle. The teacher then spins the pinwheel again, one student at a time, until all of the students in each pinwheel have had a chance to learn and to help others to learn all of the words on each student's 3 by 5 card.

It may be useful to remind students to use their six-inch voices as they help their pinwheel partners learn the spelling words. You may also want to discuss social skills and the importance of encouragement in helping others learn new skills.

Variations

The pinwheel strategy can be used as a study strategy for almost any content area that requires students to absorb a large amount of factual information. It can also be used for a brainstorming activity in which students work with partners in the pinwheel to generate ideas and solutions to problems.

To generate more movement and pinwheel effect, students in the outside circle can move a complete turn or two before stopping at their new partner. It may also be useful to allow the inside circle to alternate moving with the outside circle, preferably in the opposite direction.

Source: Adapted by Margaret Hohner, fifth grade teacher.

Informasters

Purpose

This strategy can build group relatedness through an interesting cooperative learning activity.

TARGET Areas

Task; Grouping

Grade Level

This strategy can be adapted to almost all middle and high school content areas.

Procedure

Before using this activity, expose students to several of the reference resources available in the school Learning Materials Center. You can probably arrange to have your school librarian discuss with your class the nature and uses of references like the *Dictionary of American Biography*, the *World Almanac, Visual Guide to the Natural World*, and so on.

After students are aware of the reference resources available in the LMC, divide them into groups of three or four and ask them to work together to find the answers to several "trivia hunt" questions that you have previously prepared. Students should be encouraged to work together to find the answers to the questions in the reference resources that are available.

After the groups have located and agreed upon their answers to the trivia questions, they can be challenged to browse through the reference resources to formulate four questions that can be used in another "trivia hunt." Students should be instructed to type their questions on a 3 by 5 card. They can be encouraged to name their group and include it at the top of their question card. Names like "Steve, Sally, and Sue's Sadistic Stumpers," "Brenda, Jim, and Greg's Trivia Diggers" can build group identity for this activity. On a separate card the group should type the answers to their questions and the page number and title of the reference book where each answer can be found.

Next, the class discusses their answers to the questions from the original trivia hunt and the resources they used to find their answers. On the following day or on the day that this strategy is used again, the teacher randomly distributes each group's question cards to a different group. The groups are then given a time limit to search for the answers. To avoid having several groups want to use a resource simultaneously, each group could conduct its search on an alternating period or day. Groups can then record the time that it took to find their answers, and the class can discuss the results and the difficulties they had in finding their answers. The teacher will find it useful to keep the questions for use with future classes.

Variations

This strategy can be adapted to specific courses by allowing students to use only those questions or resources that relate to science, geography, or English literature.

Students could also be encouraged to format their questions into a game such as "Jeopardy" or "College Bowl." The groups could compete against each other and use the reference resources to find the answers.

Source: Anna Moss, library media specialist.

Multicultural Celebrations

Purpose

This strategy is designed to build group relatedness and belonging by using the contributions of individual students and small groups to achieve a class goal. It also stimulates student involvement and enjoyment.

TARGET Areas

Task; Recognition; Grouping

Grade Level

This strategy is most appropriate in elementary and middle schools.

Procedure

During December, conduct a survey to identify how many different ethnic or religious groups are represented in the class, the school, or the surrounding community. Then invite the class to participate in a research project to learn about the day or days that are most significant to people in those ethnic or religious groups. For Christians the special day might be Christmas or Easter, for Jews it might be Hanukkah or Passover, for Native Americans it might be the Green Corn, Harvest, or Pow Wow celebration, for Muslims it could be Ramadan, for Vietnamese it could be Anzac Day or Tet, and so on.

Next, divide the class into groups of five or six teams and assign each team to one of the ethnic or religious groups identified in the survey. Their task is to research how the ethnic or religious group celebrates the day or days that are special to them. It is best to allow students to choose their groups, giving preference to those with first-hand information or knowledge. It may also be necessary to combine choice with random selection to ensure that all groups are equally represented.

If the community or school has more than five or six ethnic or religious groups, you can make your teams smaller or set priorities according to size. If fewer groups are represented in the community, you could set priorities by state or national constituencies.

Set aside an equal area of classroom bulletin board or wall space for each team. Inform the teams that their task is to decorate their wall space with pictures, drawings, papier-mâché objects, or other materials that show how the group they are studying celebrates their special time. You may want to encourage the teams to use their entire space, from floor to ceiling, and to be creative and colorful in their decorations. You can also invite teams to come in before or after school or during other free time to work on their decorations.

The school librarian can be a valuable resource as the teams research their ethnic or religious group. Team members can also interview students from other classes or adults in the community about how the group celebrates special days.

After all the decorations are completed, each team can give a short report to the class about their decoration and about what they have learned from their research.

4.17

Can You Top This?

Purpose

This strategy is designed to foster group relatedness by making the contributions of each participant necessary for achieving a group goal. It also stimulates student interest and enjoyment in reading while providing an opportunity for students to experience feelings of control and autonomy.

TARGET Areas

Task; Authority; Recognition; Grouping

Grade Level

This strategy is used in third grade, but can be adapted to most grade levels and content areas.

Procedure

After reading the selection "Can You Top This?" (*Connections*, Macmillan Reading Program, Level 8, Unit 2), describing a radio play, students are asked if they would like to act out the play. Some will be eager, others hesitant. Adaptions are made to the original script and a variety of committees are formed, allowing each student to participate in the drama production with a minimum of personal risk. Plans are started for organizing the production and students wanting a particular role are encouraged to audition for the part. The entire class then uses a secret ballot to vote for the students they believe will best fill each of the major parts. Some students will be pleased by the results and others may be disappointed. However, the play allows opportunities for additional actors and actresses to be added to the script. The story is about a group of youngsters taking part in a contest sponsored by a local radio station to see who can tell the best joke. This allows students to invent their own character, write their own lines (favorite joke), and by that become part of the contest, i.e., the class play. This group of students works cooperatively with the student selected for the role of announcer to coordinate their parts for the final production.

There are may opportunities for other students to work "behind the scenes." The costume committee will be busy making suggestions to actors and actresses, digging through closets and basements at home, or designing their own creations. The props committee will be searching for or constructing the necessary microphones and applause signs, in addition to designing and preparing the set. Others may prefer to work on makeup and hairstyles.

Students may choose to memorize their lines or use cue cards. Once rehearsals are under way, students can take turns sitting on the director's stool to offer suggestions like, "I can't hear you, please talk louder," or "You're talking too fast, please slow down." As the excitement grows students often ask if they may invite their parents, families, and friends to see the play. Again, additional committees are formed to issue the invitations and plan the refreshments.

Dress rehearsals are held, followed by presentations to other classrooms, and the final performance is given to invited guests. New feelings and emotions will surface from the anticipation, and they are best recognized and discussed. It is important to let students know that mistakes are of no consequence; the goal is simply to have fun together. Parents love the production, and as the students sweep up the last cookie crumb, they will likely exhibit an equal mixture of complete exhaustion and unmeasurable pride.

Variations

Other stories can easily be adapted to this format.

Source: Linda R. Johnson, Jeanne St. Marie, and Debbi Oswalt, elementary school teachers.

Stranded

Purpose

This strategy builds group relatedness and enables all students to learn decision-making skills while confronting an authentic problem-solving exercise.

TARGET Areas

Task; Authority; Grouping

Grade Level

This strategy is particularly suited for middle and high school classes.

Procedure

Begin by reading the stranded problem presented in Figure 4.9 to the class. Of the thirty items listed, ask each student to select the fifteen items he or she believes most important for survival. Then instruct the students to rank order their choices. Next, divide the class into groups of four to six students and ask the group members to discuss their choices and to try to reach consensus regarding the fifteen items their group believes most important to their survival. Explain to the class that consensus means more than just voting or that everyone must agree unanimously; it means that the group tries

FIGURE 4.9   Stranded: Problem Sheet

On vacation in July, you and your family have been travelling through the wilderness of western Maine in a pickup camper. In a blinding rainstorm you made a wrong turn on an unmarked lumber road. You have wandered more than 150 miles over a maze of lumber routes into the wilderness. The truck has run out of gas and now you, your parents, a ten-year-old sister, a six-year-old brother, and the family cat, named Charity, are lost.

After a family conference, you decide it is not wise to split up. Instead, you decide to walk back together. You are pretty sure that if you pace yourselves, you can probably cover about fifteen miles a day. Because of a fuel shortage, there are no helicopters or jeeps patrolling the area, and you have seen no other cars or houses.

The family is dressed in lightweight summer clothing and is wearing sneakers. Temperatures at night go down to the low forties. It is also bug season. As you look around you pull the following items out of the camper, some of which may be useful.

_____ fishing gear	_____ $500 in traveler's checks
_____ 44 magnum handgun & ammo	_____ 4 dacron sleeping bags
_____ matches	_____ steak (3 lbs.)
_____ marshmallows (4 bags)	_____ bug repellent
_____ walkie-talkie	_____ road map of Maine
_____ 5 gal. jug of water	_____ instant breakfast (3 boxes)
_____ house and car keys	_____ cigarettes (2 cartons)
_____ Coleman 2-burner stove	_____ family tent (10 lbs.)
_____ snakebite kit	_____ alarm clock
_____ 5 cans of kidney-liver cat food	_____ 5 lb. tub of peanut butter
_____ bathing suits	_____ 10 lb. wheel of cheese
_____ transistor radio	_____ 6 ft. tent pole
_____ sheath knife	_____ wool sweaters for everyone
_____ raft paddles	_____ inflatable rubber raft (2 pcs.; 20 lbs.)
_____ 6 paperback books	_____ first aid kit

to devise a list that satisfies all group members. This requires compromise among group members and that group members discuss each item and consider its advantages and disadvantages relative to the other items. To this end, it will be useful to review the following guidelines with your students:

1. Students should avoid arguing about their decisions. Rather, the advantages and disadvantages of each choice should be presented as clearly as possible.

2. Do not assume someone must win and someone must lose when the discussion reaches a stalemate. Look for an acceptable alternative for all.

3. Do not change your mind simply to avoid conflict and to reach agreement. Yield only to positions that have objective and logically sound foundations.

4. Avoid simple compromises like majority rule or the flip of a coin to decide an item.

5. Differences of opinion are natural and expected. Disagreement can help decision making by providing a wide range of information and opinions.

After each group reaches a consensus, distribute the following answer key to each group. (Copying it on an overhead will save paper.) Students then total the differences between their ranking of an item and the ranking provided in the answer key. For example, if an individual ranks an item as 2 and the answer key ranks it as 8, the difference is 6. The total of these differences results in the student's score. The same process is used to decide each group's score. The lower the score, the closer one is to taking the correct survival items.

After students and groups have scored their lists, conduct a class discussion of what students learned from this activity. Find out how many students' original ranking scored lower than their group's raking. (Usually the group's ranking is lower than the ranking of most individuals within the group.) Discuss the process of arriving at a group consensus and the difficulties that various groups experienced. Ask students to reflect on what they learned from this experience.

Answer Key

Rank

1 *Bug repellent*—In early summer the bugs in Maine are so fierce that they drive people mad or bite them so badly that their eyes become swollen shut.

2 *Four sleeping bags*—Full rest and warmth are essential to survival, because humans can live up to thirty days on stored fat.

3 *Tub of peanut butter*—Each tablespoon of peanut butter contains 100 calories and is high in protein.

4 *Ten-pound wheel of cheese*—Provides calcium, fats, and is an easily digestible source of protein.

5 *Steak*—A good morale booster, semiperishable. It should be eaten promptly as it is mostly protein.

6 *Transistor radio*—It's lightweight and a morale booster. Also provides useful information about weather forecasts or possible searches.

7 *Kidney-liver cat food*—A valuable if somewhat unappetizing source of protein and fat. Protein lasts longer than any other nourishment in providing energy.

8 *Matches*—Fire may be necessary to dry wet gear, boost morale, make a signal fire, and prevent serious hypothermia. It might also be used to keep animals away.

9 *Ten-pound tent*—This can be used as a place to keep warm and dry or to keep bugs out.

10 *Sheath knife*—Useful for preparing any captured animals like frogs, or cutting strings, cheese, a pole, etc.

11 *Fishing gear*—may provide a supplementary source of food. The line may be used for tying up supplies, etc.

12 *Wool sweater*—Provides lightweight warmth, wet or dry.

13 *First-aid kit*—May be helpful for minor injuries.

14 *Instant breakfast*—A lightweight source of vitamins and protein.

15 *Map*—An auto map might be useful for sighting major landmarks like lakes.

Items not taken:

16 *Marshmallows*—Not necessary, but a possible morale booster.

17 *House key*—Lightweight, but not useful for survival.

18 *Traveler's checks*—Not necessry for getting out of woods.

19 *Clock*—Not necessary for survival.

20 *Walkie-talkie*—Only useful for short-distance communication.

21 *Snakebite kit*—No poisonous snakes in Maine.

22 *Paperback books*—Weigh too much to be useful.

23 *Bathing suits*—Not necessary.

24 *Rubber raft*—Too heavy to carry and not likely to be useful.

25 *Paddles*—No use without the raft.

26 *Coleman stove*—Too heavy; wood fire can be used instead.

27 *Pole*—Knife can be used to cut a pole.

28 *44 magnum gun*—Too inaccurate for hunting. Caliber too large for small game.

29 *Five-gallon water jug*—The water in the Maine wilderness is potable.

30 *Cigarettes*—Bad for health. It's a convenient time to quit.

Variations

If time is limited, ask students to rank only five items. It is also possible to conduct the activity without ranking. In this case, simply ask students to select the fifteen most important items. Scoring can then be accomplished by adding one point for each item included on the answser key and subtracting one point for an item not included in the answer key's top fifteen.

Source: Adapted by Jean Carroll, school social worker, from: *Cowstails and Cobras* by Karl Rohnke, 1977. Copyrighted by Project Adventure, Inc. P.O. Box 100, Hamilton MA. Reprinted with permission of the publisher.

Class Photo Album

Purpose

This strategy can build positive feelings of group identity by recording and reviewing past class events. It also encourages all students to participate in expressing their thoughts and opinions about these events.

TARGET Areas

Task; Autonomy; Recognition; Grouping

Grade Level

This strategy can be adapted to almost all grade levels.

Procedure

Crate a class photographer corps by asking for volunteers from the class. Depending on the number of volunteers, a photographer for each month or two of the school year can be selected from the photographer corps. Members of the corps should have access to their own camera and have permission from their parents to bring the camera to school during the month or so that they will serve as class photographer. The teacher may decide to provide a small, inexpensive camera to be used as the class camera throughout the year. This will help control the number of photographs taken and avoid the problem of having to develop partial rolls of film from each photographer. With younger students, the teacher may choose to both supply and handle the camera.

Whenever the class participates in a special event like an assembly, listening to a guest speaker, taking a field trip, presenting small group reports, or other activities that the class considers significant, the assigned photographer takes a specified number of pictures of each event. When the film is developed, the class reviews the photos and chooses the ones that they like the best and think should be placed into the class photo album. Assign groups of two or three students to write captions for each photo. They assemble the photos and captions into the class album. A scrapbook or loose-leaf binder can be used for this purpose. Plastic inserts or lamination will help ensure that the album lasts for the full year.

The photo album can be kept in a special location in the class and shared with parents at open houses or parent-teacher conferences. It can also be shared with other classes and read at story time to younger students.

Variations

Instead of a photo album, a class newspaper could be written and illustrated with photos and articles. The photos could then be scanned into the class newspaper and copies made for each student.

Source: Suggested by Dana Thome and D. Katherine Tijerina elementary school teachers. Jones & Jones (1990).

Super Squares

Purpose

This strategy is useful for building group relatedness and for enhancing feelings of competence. It allows all students to contribute to team answers, regardless of individual abilities.

TARGET Areas

Task; Recognition; Grouping

Grade Level

This strategy can be adapted to almost all grade levels and content areas.

Procedure

After the class has completed a particular unit of study, review the unit objectives and vocabulary that students are responsible for knowing. Study guides are useful for this purpose. Next, establish a list of twenty to thirty short-answer questions from material in the study guide that focus on the unit objectives. These questions will be used to play Super Squares and they should be similar to those used in the unit exam.

To play the game, group the class into heterogeneous teams of four or five students. You can structure the groups according to previous test scores or you can form the groups randomly or use a grouping strategy similar to the one suggested in Strategy 4.6. Each group selects a team spokesperson, but the group members work together to establish a consensus for each decision.

Write the numbers 1 through the number of groups on slips of paper and fold them in half. Shake the slips in your hand and have each group spokesperson select a slip. Slip numbers determine the order in which teams play the game. When called on, each team decides through consensus which number to select from the game board (see Figure 4.10). The teacher then reads a question from the prepared list and the team discusses the question and uses a consensus to arrive at an answer for the team spokesperson. If the spokesperson gives the correct answer, the team is awarded the selected square. Each team can use a different colored marker to cross out the numbers of awarded squares. Incorrect answers are not penalized, but the selected square is left open. The question can then be moved to the bottom of the list and used later. The

FIGURE 4.10 Super Squares

9	16	2	29	13
20	1	25	8	28
7	23	10	17	12
15	26	19	3	30
4	11	6	24	21
22	14	27	18	5

winning team is the first to get three adjacent horizontal, vertical, or diagonal squares.

The game board can be made into a laminated chart or into a transparency to be used with an overhead projector. Students enjoy playing the game, and it provides an excellent review before an exam.

Variations

Students can be encouraged to write their own questions for use in the game. These can be written on three by five cards and assigned a day or two before the game is played. The teacher then collects the cards and uses them for the question bank.

Rather than announce aloud what number the team is selecting, they can write it on a slip of paper. If the question is answered correctly, the number is read to the class and the corresponding square is awarded. If the question is answered incorrectly, the following team can choose to answer the question correctly and get the unknown square selected by the previous team, or they can select their own number and a new question.

Source: Patricia Kreil, elementary school teacher.

CHAPTER FIVE

Strategies for Enhancing Student Self-Esteem

Self-esteem has been defined as appreciating one's own worth and importance, having the character to be accountable for oneself, and acting responsibly toward others (Reasoner, 1982). Students with high self-esteem are more likely to succeed in life because they have a clear sense of direction regarding their priorities and their goals. They can reflect on their plans and aspirations, and then take the necessary steps to achieve success. Therefore, it seems reasonable that activities designed to increase students' self-esteem will also increase their intrinsic motivation to learn.

RECOMMENDATIONS FOR INCREASING STUDENT SELF-ESTEEM IN THE CLASSROOM

1. *Set high expectations for all students and assist students in achieving them.* Students will rise or fall to the level of expectation of their teachers. When teachers believe in students, students believe in themselves.

2. *Provide all students with ample amounts of positive information feedback.* Information feedback describes students' achievements, skills, or social behaviors. It also avoids value judgments.

3. *Always try to explain the reason or purpose for rules, assignments, and learning activities.* Only if you draw attention to the value of activities will your students experience the personal satisfaction that comes with achieving them.

4. *Learn something unique about each student and occasionally mention it to them.*

5. *Value students' efforts as well as their accomplishments.* Hard work, whatever its outcome needs to be appreciated and reinforced. Teachers must also match tasks to the skill level of the student, so that effort can lead to success.

6. *Help students learn to accept their mistakes and successes by occasionally modeling an analysis of your own errors and achievements.* Modeling self-talk that demonstrates your acceptance of mistakes or reinforces your achievements helps students appreciate their own strengths and limitations (e.g., "It looks as if I have added incorrectly; I'll have to be more careful next time," or "I feel wonderful about today's lesson; I worked hard preparing it, and everyone met the objectives."

7. *Accept students as valuable, worthwhile human beings, although you may have to reject particular behaviors.* Students are not bad, inconsiderate, or mean because of what they do; although, at times, specific behavior may be all of those things. It is important to distinguish between what a student does and what a student is.

8. *Celebrate the accomplishments and achievements of all students.* "We can complain because rose bushes have thorns, or we can rejoice because thorn bushes have roses." We must see through student misbehaviors to find accomplishments that we can acknowledge and support.

9. *Encourage students to evaluate their behavior relative to their goals and prior level of achievement.* Students experience genuine success when they make progress along the path that leads to clearly defined goals.

10. *Create a psychologically safe climate in which students are encouraged to express their opinions and risk being different.* Classroom environments must protect the dignity and security of all who inhabit them; teachers must be firm and consistent.

3-D Self-Portrait Box

Purpose

The purpose of this activity is to enhance students' self-esteem by encouraging them to identify and share their individual attributes, beliefs, and experiences in a symbolic three-dimensional format.

TARGET Areas

Task; Authority; Recognition

Grade Level

This strategy can be adapted to art classes at almost all grade levels.

Procedure

Start this activity with a discussion of student differences and how these differences can make people more interesting. Then tell the class that they are going to construct three-dimensional portraits that demonstrate the differences among the students in the class.

Encourage students to find or construct a box that can hold a three-dimensional collage that will give the viewer an insight into the personality of the artist. The boxes can take a variety of forms (open, closed, cutaway, etc.), and should have minimum dimensions of 12"(H) ×

12"(W) × 6"(D). The only limit on maximum size is that the box must fit through the classroom door (this statement will allow students to expand their thinking about the project).

Encourage students to use any material they prefer to construct their collage within the box. Their task is to enable the viewer to understand the artist's likes, dislikes, hobbies, previous experiences, aspirations, role models, heroes, and so on. The more the artist includes in the presentation, the better he or she will be understood.

Inform students that the evaluation of the project will be done privately by the teacher and the student at the end of the unit. The principles of composition and design will comprise the largest weighting for the final grade. (The teacher may want to prepare an evaluation checklist to give to students before they start the project.) The teacher will want to encourage students to think beyond magazine pictures quickly glued to the box the night before the project is due. Students should consider using materials like photos, keys, CD covers, paint, fabric, wire, metal, plastic, clay, Styrofoam, animal or vegetable products that will not decay, and any other memorabilia that will contribute to their self-portrait.

It is important to give all students an opportunity to discuss their final portrait with others in the class. This can be accomplished in small groups or by allowing a portion of the class to mingle among the boxes with the artists available to provide explanations.

Variations

Teachers can use hanging collages or poster board instead of boxes to convey the self-portrait.

Source: Jane Conover, high school art teacher.

5.2

Ugly Ducklings

Purpose

This strategy builds self-esteem and feelings of competence by encouraging students to overcome their weaknesses and to build on their strengths.

TARGET Areas

Task; Recognition

Grade Level

This strategy can be adapted to almost all grade levels and content areas.

Procedure

With elementary students, the teacher should start by reading to the class Hans Christian Anderson's tale of the *Ugly Duckling*. Then the teacher should ask students to share with the class activities that they do well. Instead of focusing on obvious academic, athletic, or musical talents, the teacher might want to help students focus on hidden talents. For example, students often care for younger siblings, keep a garden or plants, cook meals or make desserts, take care of pets, or other such tasks. After discussing these talents, ask the students to make a collage of photos, pictures, or drawings that showcase their hidden talents. These can be hung in the classroom and shared with others.

With middle or secondary school students, the teacher can generate student interest and curiosity by reading the following biographical sketches and asking students to guess the person being described:

Sketch 1

As a child, other kids made fun of me because I stuttered a lot when I spoke and I also had a bad lisp. I was not a very good student in school and my scores were often the lowest in my class. My father was a well known politician and lecturer, but most people thought that I was not smart enough to follow in his footsteps. Who am I?

Answer: Winston Churchill, *prime minister of England during World War II, and winner of the Nobel Prize for literature.*

Sketch 2

I was always a good student in school, but I would often get angry when I couldn't do something perfectly the first time. Teachers and my friends called me a perfectionist. When I was younger, I had a problem with motion sickness. I even became queasy when I rode my hobbyhorse. As a teenager, I would often get sick on carnival rides or long car trips. Who am I?

Answer: Christa McAuliffe, *the first schoolteacher to be selected from more than 10,000 applicants to become an astronaut on a space mission.*

Sketch 3

When I was in school, teachers didn't like me because they thought I asked too many silly questions. One teacher thought that there was something wrong with the way my mind worked. Because of this, my mother took me out of school and taught me at home. I never returned to school.

Answer: Thomas Edison, *inventor of the first record player, electric light bulb, and numerous other conveniences.*

Sketch 4

When I was a child my parents thought something was wrong with me because I didn't learn to speak until I was six years old. I also took a long time to answer when people asked me questions. Some thought that I was strange and unfriendly and would never make a success of anything. Who am I?

Answer: Albert Einstein, *Nobel Prize-winning scientist and philosopher who proposed the theory of relativity.*

186

Sketch 5

When I was a child, my parents made me take piano lessons, but I often skipped so that I could play ball with my friends. During one recital, I embarrassed my family by being the only student that didn't know his part. Whom am I?

Answer: Duke Ellington, *famous jazz musician, band leader, and composer.*

Sketch 6

I didn't learn to read until I was ten years old. I was twelve when I started school, and I was always behind in my studies. I was especially poor in math and could never memorize facts very well. I had difficulty getting along with other kids in my grade, and older boys would pick fights with me. Who am I?

Answer: Woodrow Wilson, *president of the United States during World War I.*

Depending on the course and grade level, teachers can explain that in spite of the problems that these individuals experienced in school or with others, they all became successful adults. Ask students if they know or have heard of other people with similar experiences. Students can also be encouraged to read about the early lives of these famous individuals and share additional findings with the class.

Variations

In art classes, students can be encouraged to draw pictures or make collages that incorporate both the early and later lives of these celebrities. Since people grow and learn in unique ways, students may want to reflect on their individual paths to success. By anticipating the obstacles that they may experience along the way, they can plan for the supports that they will need to overcome them.

Source: Adapted from Suzanne Roush, elementary teacher; *Learning88,* September poster.

Put-Ups

Purpose

This strategy enhances the self-esteem of both the giver and the receiver. It can also build a sense of group relatedness by focusing on positive interactions among members of the class.

TARGET Areas

Authority; Recognition

Grade Level

This strategy works best with elementary students, but could be adapted to middle school.

Procedure

A section of the bulletin board or wall space is set aside for the duration of the school year for "put-ups." (A put-up is a positive statement or comment given to a student by a classmate who observed the student doing a positive or helpful behavior. They are the opposites of put-downs.) To help students use put-ups, the teacher places a small box near the bulletin board containing forms for students to complete (see Figure 5.1) when they want to give a classmate a put-up.

FIGURE 5.1   Put-Ups

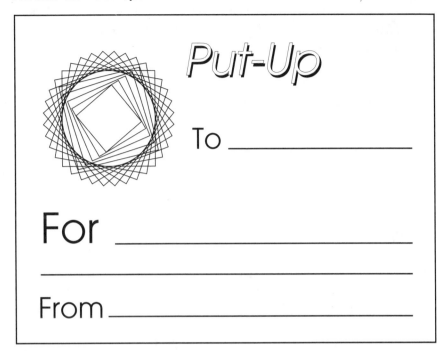

Students should be encouraged to fill out a form each time they hear a classmate saying a positive statement or observe a classmate behaving positively toward others. Both anonymous and signed put-ups should be available.

The teacher should take care when introducing this activity to ensure that students understand what constitutes an appropriate put-up. The activity should not turn into a popularity contest. Good put-ups should be specific about the behavior or statement being commended. An appropriate put-up, for example, might be, "It was nice of you to help a first grader zip up her coat at recess this morning." An inappropriate put-up would be a general statement such as, "Thank you for being a nice person."

Variations

Students could present their put-ups directly to the person being commended rather than post them on the bulletin board. Put-ups could also be placed in a special box to ensure anonymity, and opened during a specific time of the week.

Teachers might also want to fill out anonymous put-ups and place them in the mailboxes of colleagues they hear making positive statements or observe behaving positively toward others.

Source: Susan Kjelstrup, elementary school teacher.

Name Bugs

Purpose

This strategy builds self-esteem and relatedness by helping students get to know each other and to see themselves as unique members of a group.

TARGET Areas

Task; Recognition; Grouping

Grade Level

This strategy is best used with elementary and middle school students.

Procedure

At the beginning of the school year (or any time new groups of students are brought together) the teacher opens with a discussion about making new friends and getting to know the people around them. Next, the teacher asks students to think about the interests and talents that each has and that they might be willing to share with their classmates. After the discussion, a piece of drawing paper (both 9" × 12" and 12" × 18" work well) is distributed to each student. The teacher then asks the students to make a lengthwise fold on their paper and to write (not print) their first names in large lowercase letters about one-quarter inch above the fold (see Figure 5.2).

FIGURE 5.2 Name Bug

    Leaving their paper folded, students are instructed to go to a window to trace a mirror image of their name on the other side of the fold. They are then instructed to unfold their papers and to connect the two names to form a "name bug." (The teacher may want to demonstrate this with his or her name.)

Students can be encouraged to use colored pencils, crayons, or magic markers, to add details that represent their hobbies, interests, and talents (tennis rackets, musical notes, baseball bats, favorite colors, etc.), They can also be encouraged to add eyes, extra legs, feelers, and tails to showcase their uniqueness and to make an interest piece of art. When the bugs are completed, the students can carefully cut out the bugs with scissors.

When all students have finished constructing their name bugs, the teacher places each student with a partner and asks them to discuss their name bugs. After the pairs have exchanged information, each student should introduce his or her partner to the class and share what they have learned. When all students have had a turn, the name bugs can be displayed on a bulletin board. A construction paper flower garden made by the students makes a colorful backdrop for the display.

Variations

Teachers could use the information from the bulletin board bugs to further help students get to know each other. They could challenge the class to "find someone who likes karate" or to "name three people in the class who play a musical instrument."

Source: Katy Grogan, middle school teacher.

Life Line

Purpose

This activity can help develop positive self-esteem by increasing students' awareness of their significant positive life experiences.

TARGET Areas

Task; Authority; Recognition

Grade Level

This strategy can be adapted to almost all grade levels and content areas.

Procedure

Introduce this activity by asking your students to recall events from their past that have generated positive feelings for them. Request that each class member make a list of these events by writing down as many as they can remember. Encourage students to start with their early memories, writing down things that come to mind as they move from year to year in their past. The teacher can help by asking the class members to focus on positive experiences in sports, math, reading, art, music, working at home, summer experiences, helping parents or neighbors, baby sitting, or family trips and vacations. The teacher can also ask students to think about events when they laughed, when they felt proud, when they were successful, or when they had to make important decisions. After students have finished, have them review their lists and select what they believe are the eight most important events.

Depending on the grade level, the teacher can ask the group to use construction paper and art materials to draw 6" × 6" picture representing each experience. After they have finished with their drawings, they can arrange the pictures in chronological order and then punch a hole in the top corner of each picture. Next, using an eight-foot length of string or yarn, students can "thread" each picture on what is about to become their personal life line. (Prevent the pictures from sliding by tying a small knot before and after each picture as they are strung on the line.)

When the life lines are finished, each student should be given an opportunity to describe his or her positive chronology to a partner, a small group, or to the entire class. The students can then mount their life lines along the walls of the classroom.

Older students might prefer to draw a life line on a piece of construction paper with their birth date on one end and the current date on the other. They can use a combination of sketches or descriptive statements to identify the eight significant events along the chronology. Students can then share their life lines with a partner or in a small group.

Variations

The number of events used in the life line can vary according to the preferences of the teacher or the group. Rather than drawing pictures, some individuals may prefer to cut pictures that represent their positive events from old magazines.

In addition to focusing on positive events, the teacher could encourage students to identify any event that was significant or important in their lives. In this case, it is important that the group be supportive, since these events may involve divorce or the loss of a family member.

Similarity Wheels

Purpose

This two-part activity can enhance student self-esteem and build a sense of group relatedness among class members.

TARGET Areas

Task; Recognition

Grade Level

This strategy is especially useful in elementary and middle schools, but can be adapted to almost all grade levels and content areas.

Procedure

Make a similarity wheel (see Figure 5.3) for each student by drawing a large circle on a sheet of paper. Then draw a smaller, two-inch diameter circle in the middle of the larger circle. Next, divide the larger circle into eight equally sized sections by drawing eight lines from the outside of the inner circle to the edge of the larger circle. Finally, write a statement in each section of the newly created wheel that students can finish by writing some information about themselves (Figure 5.3 provides some examples of these questions.)

FIGURE 5.3 Similarity Wheels

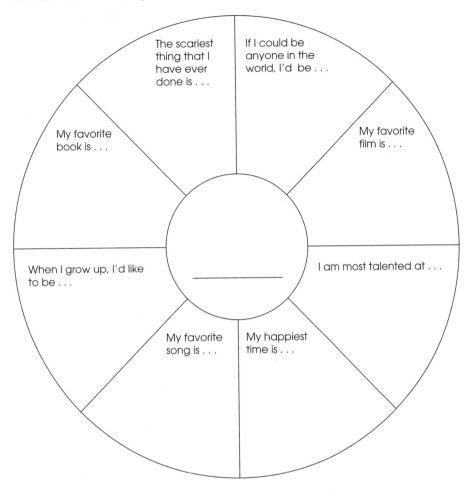

The scariest thing that I have ever done is . . .

If I could be anyone in the world, I'd be . . .

My favorite book is . . .

My favorite film is . . .

When I grow up, I'd like to be . . .

I am most talented at . . .

My favorite song is . . .

My happiest time is . . .

Distribute the wheels and ask the students to complete each statement in the space provided. Encourage them to use no more than half of the space allocated for each question. When all students are finished, ask them to write their name on the line in the middle of the smaller circle. Collect the wheels and save the second part of this activity for the following day.

On the next day, give the wheels back to the students and ask them to walk around the class to see if they can find others with answers identical or similar to theirs. When a match is found, each student should sign the other's wheel in the matching segment.

When all students have had an opportunity to check each other's answers, ask the students to return to their seats. When the class is ready, ask students to share the answers to questions that provided many matches and those that were unique or had few matches. These responses can be used to focus a discussion on sameness and uniqueness in different people.

Variations

This strategy can be used as an ice-breaking activity for new groups of students. Here, the teacher may want to do both parts of the activity during the same class period.

Teachers can vary the type of questions asked in each segment of the wheel. The teacher might want to use questions that help them focus on different monthly themes in the lives of their students.

Source: Suggested by Linda Schoenbeck, elementary school teacher.

My Me Book

Purpose

This strategy can help students develop a sense of personal identity and uniqueness while encouraging self-expression.

TARGET Areas

Task; Authority; Recognition

Grade Level

This strategy is most useful in elementary grades.

Procedure

This strategy encourages each student to construct a "Me Book" composed of stories, pictures, and illustrations that document important examples of each child's uniqueness. The book can be entitled "My Me Book," and can include a picture of the student on the cover. Each page of the book requires students to think and write about a certain feature or aspect of themselves. With younger students, it can consist of responses and illustrations to lead-in phrases that focus on topics like my parents, my grandparents, my brothers and sisters, my friends, the proud me, the frightened me, the happy me, my neighbors, my hobbies, my music, or my aspirations. Each page can start with a phrase such as, "My brother _____ ," "I get mad when _____ ," or "My favorite song is _____ ." Students write responses to complete each sentence and illustrate their responses with family pictures, pictures from magazines, or pictures they draw. Pages can be stored by the teacher or placed in a folder so that they can be compiled into book form at the end of the exercise.

Teachers can extend this project over one or two weeks or it can be an ongoing project that continues to grow throughout the year. The final product can be shared with the class and then brought home and shared with the student's family.

Variations

Lead-in phrases can be adapted to the age of the student. Older students can be encouraged to write several sentences or a paragraph about a lead-in phrase. Some teachers may want to eliminate lead-in phrases to allow students maximum flexibility to turn their Me Books into autobiographies that include favorite poems, significant life experiences, favorite memories, or other experiences that convey the student's uniqueness.

Source: Suggested by Lori Pfeiffer and Sally VanBrocklin, elementary school teachers.

Stick-On Encouragers

Purpose

This strategy can help build positive self-esteem and feelings of competence.

TARGET Areas

Task; Recognition; Grouping; Evaluation

Grade Level

This strategy will be demonstrated in a middle school English class, but it can be adapted to almost all grade levels and content areas.

Procedure

This strategy can be used when students are given almost any writing assignment. It is especially valuable when students are asked to write creative short stories. After all students have completed their writing assignment, divide the class into groups of four or five students. Give all students a pad of small stick-on note slips and a pencil. Instruct students to read their papers to their groups. Group members can be encouraged to take notes on a separate sheet of paper. When a student finishes reading a paper, the group discusses the writing and asks any questions that they may have for the writer. Next, using a stick-on note slip, each student writes two or three *positive and encouraging* phrases or sentences about the story and how it was written. The student that read the story then passes his or her paper around the group and each group member sticks their note slip of encouraging remarks to the back of the student's story. The stories are kept in a pile until all of the readers have finished. They are then returned to their writers, and each will now have slips of positive and encouraging comments about their story to read at their leisure.

Variations

The teacher may decide to collect each group's pile of stories before they are returned to the writers. This will allow the teacher to add his or her own feedback to the writer while commenting on the group members' reactions.

Source: Rosemary Walsh, middle school English teacher; Brenda O'Beirne, counselor educator.

The Day You Were Born

Purpose

This strategy supports self-esteem by providing students with an opportunity to feel proud of themselves. It also helps them gain confidence and skill in using library resources.

TARGET Areas

Task; Recognition

Grade Level

This strategy is especially useful for middle and high school language arts and English classes.

Procedure

This strategy is best used with a class visit to a large local, regional, or state library that has an extensive microform library. Students are given the task of researching the significant things that happened on the day they were born. They can be assigned to include information from at least three newspapers—the local paper from the town or city where they were born (if none is available, they can use the closest large city), the paper from the largest or closest city to their birthplace, and the *New York Times*.

Encourage students to take notes about the local, state, national, and international issues and incidents that were taking place as they were entering the world. They should also read the papers to get a sense of the popular culture. What were the clothes fashions or hairstyles of the time? How much did things cost? Who were the winning sports teams? What were the popular TV programs or movies?

After students return to their classroom, they can be encouraged to write and "publish" the front page and society page of a newspaper about the day they were born. The front page could include information from their research of previously published papers that would give the reader a sense of the time. On the society page they can write third-person "predictions" about their life, based on their current interests and accomplishments. These might take the form of "Joe Jones, born on this cold, windy day, will some day become a starting center for the Fighting Tigers basketball team and average 12 points and 13 assists per game during his sophomore year," or "When this fair-haired baby Melissa is in her twenties, she will be instrumental in eliminating world hunger . . . " Students could include cartoons that depict the time, or letters to the editor ("I am writing to thank Joe Jones's parents for having such a wonderful son . . . ").

Variations

This strategy could be accomplished using just the resources of the school or local library. Students could also be encouraged to use school computers and desktop publishing programs to produce the pages of their "newspaper." This might allow the possibility of scanning in baby pictures, birth certificates, or footprints to personalize each "newspaper."

Source: Anna Moss, library media center director.

Through the Gender Looking Glass

Purpose

This strategy is designed to break down some of the hidden gender and racial hierarchies in classrooms and to enhance the self-esteem of all students.

TARGET Areas

Task; Authority; Recognition

Grade Level

This strategy can be adapted to almost all grade levels and content areas.

Procedure

This strategy is best conducted as part of an American history unit or class in which students are asked to research the lives of prominent Americans (living or dead) and perform brief dramatic monologues as those individuals. However, with this strategy, students are required to prepare two presentations, one as a male and the other as a female.

Girls have little difficulty with this assignment, but boys, especially in middle school, may have some problems with the required shift in mind-set. They may protest the assignment and make disparaging remarks about having to play a girl or woman. It is important, therefore, that teachers establish a supportive but serious atmosphere for conducting the research and monologues. The originator of this strategy, Ms. Judy Logan, a middle school teacher in San Francisco, found that since the two roles were required, the boys in her class accepted the assignment without question, although they would be unlikely to choose female roles on their own.

The teacher should encourage the class to be creative and theatrical in presenting their monologues. They should also be encouraged to use costumes, music, and props to help dramatize the productions. Teachers should have as many resources as possible available for students to use as they select their characters and plan their productions. Early planning with the school librarian or media coordinator should help in obtaining additional books and resources from sources outside the school. The more effort students put into selecting their character and planning their presentations, the more likely they will stay in character throughout their monologue.

Nervous giggling and laughing will often accompany presentations from boys who are unaccustomed to playing a feminine role. It is important that the teacher encourage them to take the role seriously rather than making a mockery of it. Asking the character questions about his or her life and experiences can help reduce some of the nervousness. Videotaping presentations for sharing with parents or other classes can also contribute to a more thoughtful atmosphere. Student autonomy can be supported by allowing individuals the option of reciting their monologue alone with the teacher rather than in front of the class.

After the presentations, the teacher can conduct a discussion of the feelings that students experienced playing their male and female roles. Issues of gender discrimination, stereotyping, and bias can be addressed from a point of view seldom experienced by students.

Variations

The activity can be used in an African American history class or during African American history week. Students are required to perform dramatic monologues as prominent male and female African Americans (past or present).

Source: Adapted from Judy Logan, middle school teacher, as described in Orenstein, P. (1994). *School girls: Young women, self-esteem, and the confidence gap.* New York: Doubleday.

Random Acts of Kindness

Purpose

This strategy can build self-esteem by encouraging students to reflect on the importance of treating others with the kindness and consideration that they want for themselves.

TARGET Areas

Task; Authority; Recognition

Grade Level

This strategy can be adapted to almost all grade levels and content areas.

Procedure

Figure 5.4 provides a list of famous quotes that emphasize the importance of kindness and consideration in interpersonal relationships. Reproduce those items on this list that are appropriate to the reading and comprehension level of your students. Write your list on the chalkboard, an overhead, or on a handout for all students. Begin this strategy by asking each student to select the one quote that they like the most and that conveys what they believe to be an important and valuable message. After students have made their selections, ask those that have selected quote number 1

FIGURE 5.4 Quotable Quotes

"No one is useless in the world who lightens the burden of it for anyone else."
—Charles Dickens

"Do unto others as you would have them do unto you." —The Golden Rule

"Kindness is the oil that takes the friction out of life." —Anonymous

"What you are speaks so loudly, I can't hear what you are saying."
—Ralph Waldo Emerson

"Practice random, useless acts of kindness." —Anonymous

"Speak kind words and you will hear kind echoes." —Henry George Bohn

"The best portion of a good man's life are his little, nameless, unremembered acts
of kindness and of love." —William Wordsworth

"You cannot do a kindness too soon, for you never know how soon it will be too
late." —Ralph Waldo Emerson

"Kindness is a language the dumb can speak and the deaf can hear and understand." —Christian Nestell Bovee

"Those who bring sunshine to the lives of others cannot keep it from themselves."
—Sir James Barrie

to go to one part of the room, those that have selected number 2 to a different part of the room, an so on until there are as many groups as quotes. Groups that are larger than four or five students should be randomly subdivided. If only one student has selected a particular quotation, he or she should be encouraged to select a second choice.

Ask each group to form a circle, and each member to take a turn discussing what the quotation means to them and why they selected it over the others. After all members have an opportunity to talk about the quotation, ask the group to brainstorm a list of ways that they could put the idea conveyed by the quotation into practice in their classroom. They should be encouraged to focus on the specific behaviors that would show the message of the quotation in as much detail as possible. When the groups have exhausted their ideas, they should discuss their lists so that each member of the group understands the types of behaviors that show the kindness conveyed in their quotation. Each student should then select one of the acts of kindness from their group's list that he or she can demonstrate during the coming week.

Next, the teacher writes each student's name on a slip of paper and each class member draws a slip without letting others see the name. During the following week, each student is asked to show their act of kindness with the student they selected. Students should be encouraged to show their kindness without the others being aware of when they do it. The groups can meet the following week and discuss how they felt giving and receiving kindness.

Variations

Depending on the age level of the group, several variations for carrying out the kindness behaviors are possible. Students can show their act of kindness behavior with students of their choice or they can be asked to show it with several different students throughout the week. The small group discussions following the acts of kindness can be expanded to include a full class discussion of how it felt giving and receiving an act of kindness. Students can also discuss the artificiality of the exercise and what they can do to show acts of kindness more genuinely.

The Gender Journey

Purpose

This strategy is designed to build the self-esteem of all students by encouraging them to develop a sensitivity to gender differences.

TARGET Areas

Task; Authority

Grade Level

This strategy can be adapted to almost all grade levels and content areas.

Procedure

This strategy uses imagery to take students back in time and to experience their lives from a different frame of reference. Announce to your class that they are going to take a journey back in time. Ask the students to sit comfortably in their desks; some may choose to put their heads down and to keep their eyes closed throughout the journey. Instruct them to breathe a little deeper than normal and as they exhale, to feel themselves relaxing more and more in their desks.

When the class has settled down and students are sitting quietly with their eyes closed, ask them to forget everything around them and to imagine that they are back to their previous year's classroom. (Sixth grade students will be used in this example.) Ask students to try to see themselves sitting in their fifth-grade desks. Encourage them to remember how the room looked, what they were wearing, who was sitting next to them, and who was their best friend. Give the students about ten seconds to recreate this picture in their mind's eye.

Continuing the journey backward in time, ask students to see themselves in their third grade class. They should try to picture their teacher and what she was wearing. Again, they should try to see who was sitting next to them and who was their best friend. After a few seconds, ask students to see themselves going home after school in third grade. How did they get there? Who was with them? Ask them to see themselves in their room at home. What kinds of toys and books did they have? How was their room decorated?

After another ten or twenty seconds, ask students to try to see themselves on the first day of kindergarten. How did they look? What were they wearing? What did they enjoy doing? Continue to journey backward to their first preschool memories. Who did they play with? What were their favorite toys?

After taking students back to their early memories, ask them to try to imagine the day that they were born. Have them envision the excitement on their parents' faces. Next, ask students to imagine that each was born the *opposite sex*.

Some students may gasp or make negative comments at this suggestion, but persist in encouraging students to move forward on the backward path they have been following. Take the group back to the same situations again, giving them time to view each environment from a different gender. What would their classrooms or bedrooms look like? What kinds of toys or clothes would they have? Who would be their friends? What kinds of books would they read?

After giving the class the same amount of time on the return trip as was taken on the backward trip, ask the class to slowly open their eyes and return to their classroom and original gender. Although there will likely be many nervous side comments, ask students to save their remarks for a few minutes, take out a sheet of paper, and list all the things (not to be collected) that would be different in their lives if they were born the opposite sex.

Finally, conduct a class discussion of the students' lists. This can be facilitated by writing the words MALES and FEMALES across the top of the chalkboard or on butcher paper taped to the wall. As students discuss items from their lists, the teacher can write down their comments under the appropriate columns. During this process, students can be encouraged to discuss how their lives were different on the return journey. It is important to allow students to pass and keep their lists to themselves, if they so choose.

After both lists are filled, the teacher can ask students to judge the accuracy of the opposite sex's perception of their gender. Students should be encouraged to avoid defensiveness as they point out discrepancies between their experiences and others' perceptions or assumptions.

Encourage students to scrutinize the two lists to see if the comments for one gender are more disparaging than for the other. Ask students to discuss the implications of their observations and what can be done to ensure that both genders are treated equally in their school and classroom.

Variations

Instead of using a guided recall, teachers might ask students to write an impromptu or assigned theme on the gender switch topic. However, this experience will not usually produce the emotional identification generated by a guided recall.

Teachers might also incorporate some results of the AAUW survey of the attitudes and opinions of three thousand boys and girls between the ages of nine and fifteen (Orenstein, 1994). Most shocking are the data that show a dramatic loss in self-esteem and perceptions of competence for girls as they approach adolescence. Particularly interesting are the ethnic differences found in the study and reported by Orenstein:

> *Far more African American girls retain their overall self-esteem during adolescence than white or Latina girls, maintaining a stronger sense of both personal and familial importance. They are about twice as likely to be "happy with the way I am" than girls of other groups and report feeling "pretty good at a lot of things" at nearly the rate of white boys. (1994, xvii)*

Source: Adaptd from Judy Logan, middle school teacher, as described in Orenstein, P. (1994). *School girls: Young women, self-esteem, and the confidence gap.* New York: Doubleday.

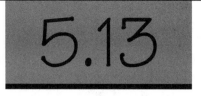

Silent Solutions

Purpose

This strategy builds feelings of self-esteem and competence by encouraging students to communicate solutions to problems nonverbally. Since students are prohibited from talking, they do not have to worry about saying something stupid or embarrassing.

TARGET Areas

Task; Authority; Recognition; Grouping

Grade Level

This strategy can be adapted to almost all grade levels and content areas.

Procedure

Divide the class into groups of four to six students. Select one of the following problem situations and ask each group member to try to think of a solution to the problem. When they think that they have one, their task is to pantomime or act out their solution in front of their group. When the student has finished and others in the group recognize the solution, other group members with different solutions can continue the role play. It is important to emphasize that talking is prohibited throughout the solution demonstration.

All students should be given an opportunity to nonverbally demonstrate a solution. When everyone has had an opportunity to act out an answer, group members can choose their most creative or original solution to demonstrate in front of the class.

It is important to provide an opportunity for all students to pantomime in front of their group. To achieve this end, no student should be given a second opportunity to pantomime until all the others in their group have had a chance to participate.

Problem Situations:

1. You are at a theme park with your parents and a friend. After you and your friend exit your first ride, you realize that you cannot find your parents. You did not make any prearrangement for this possibility and neither you nor your friend remember where the car was parked. Your parents were holding all of the ride tickets.

2. You are camping with your parents. Your parents are sleeping in the camper and you and your brother are sleeping in a small tent. During the middle of the night, you are awakened by a scratching noise outside the tent near your head.

3. You are sledding on a hill near your home with some friends. You ask a friend if you can try a run with his newer and faster sled. As you are coming down the hill, you lose control and run into a tree. You are not hurt, but the runner on your friend's sled is broken.

4. You are talking with a classmate on the playground, and you get hit in the back of the head by a snowball. You turn around and see a group of students from a different class nearby, but you can't tell which one threw the snowball.

5. You are waiting to check out a book in the library, and an older and bigger student cuts in front of you.

6. As you are eating your lunch in the school cafeteria, two younger students seem angry and start pushing each other.

7. You have a book report due the next day, but cannot find a tablet or pad of paper.

8. You are biking with a friend several miles from home and your rear tire blows out.

9. You are in the middle of mixing up a batch of cookies for a bake sale and realize that you do not have a cookie sheet for baking them.

10. You have some friends visiting and as you are watching a rented video, the tape breaks in the middle.

Variations

It may be possible to design problem situations that deal with the subjects students are studying. In social studies, for example, students might try to solve a problem faced by Lewis or Clark during their expedition, or in reading, students might pantomime a different ending to a story they have read.

Care Cards

Purpose

This strategy enhances self-esteem by allowing students to draw a picture of something they care about and share it with others in the class.

TARGET Areas

Task; Authority; Recognition

Grade Level

This strategy is particularly useful in elementary grades.

Procedure

Distribute a 5 × 8 index card to students in the class and ask them to draw a picture of someone or something that they care about very much. They can draw a picture of anything that is important or meaningful to them and that they would like to share with the class. If students have difficulty drawing the person or article they care about, tell them that they can draw a symbol to represent their object. When students have finished, collect the cards and use them to decorate the classroom by pinning them to the bulletin board or taping them along the top of the chalk board. Give each student an opportunity to explain their card to the class.

As students discuss the cared-for object, ask them to identify ways that they show their caring. If the object is a pet dog, for example, have them explain how they show their dog that it is loved. They might also want to comment on how frequently they show their caring.

Students seem to enjoy this simple activity. They discover that many in the class care for the same things (pets seem to dominate), and that they often forget to show their caring. The strategy can also build feelings of belonging as students listen to each other and learn to accept what is important to each of them.

Variations

Many variations of this strategy are possible. Drawing paper can be used instead of index cards, and an entire wall of the classroom can be decorated with the finished pictures. Students could also use their drawing as a cover for a short story about the person or thing they care about. In the story they could discuss why they care about the object or person and how they show their caring. Besides parents and pets, the class can be encouraged to draw other objects or people that they care about.

Resident Specialists

Purpose

This strategy helps students identify their strengths. It also provides them with a list of students who can serve as resources when they have difficulty with a task or learning a new skill.

TARGET Areas

Authority; Recognition

Grade Level

This strategy is most appropriate in elementary grades.

Procedure

Ask students to identify two or three skills or tasks that they do especially well, and that they would be willing to help others learn to do more effectively. Tell students that the skill can be from any area they prefer and might include things like throwing a football, hitting a softball, swimming the backstroke, writing letters, printing neatly, baking bread, ironing, adding fractions, finding least common denominators, cross country skiing, fishing, knitting, fixing flat tires on bikes, using computer programs, or tying decorative knots.

Collect the lists and compile an alphabetical tabulation of the skill areas followed by the names of students who identified themselves as a specialist in the area. Type the directory of specialists and distribute a copy to each student. Also, place a copy of the directory on the class bulletin board. It can become a valuable resource for students who would like assistance with improving their skills in an area.

Explain to students that although it's not always easy to ask for help from other students, the purpose of the specialist directory is to provide them with the names of classmates who could be willing to help them in any area they choose. It is also useful for the teacher to conduct a class discussion of the characteristics of effective helpers. Students can be asked to list these characteristics on a chalkboard and then discuss the difficulties that they might have in showing them. The discussion could also focus on the importance of saying thanking you when assitance is given, and how it might feel to receive a thank you note from another student.

It is important to ensure that all students are listed under at least one area of the Resident Specialist list. Also, it is useful to update the list once or twice a semester so that students have an opportunity to add new areas of expertise to the list.

Variations

The Resident Specialist list might be shared with other classes at the same or at different grade levels. Younger students, particularly, find it useful to seek out specialists in a grade or two above them. It may be helpful if teachers schedule specific times for students of lower grades to consult with specialists from upper grades.

Source: Adapted from Jones & Jones (1990).

Name and Body Acrostic

Purpose

This strategy fosters feelings of self-esteem by providing students with an opportunity to give and receive positive statements related to letters in their name, and it supports physical awareness through body images.

TARGET Areas

Task; Recognition; Grouping

Grade Level

This strategy is appropriate for all elementary grades.

Procedure

An acrostic is a poem in which the first letter of the lines, read downward, forms a word or phrase. The strategy uses an acrostic designed around each student's name.

Divide the class into groups of three or four students. Ask the groups to measure the height of each of its members and to total the numbers in inches and feet (metric units may be used). Using a large roll of butcher or wrapping paper (contact the art teacher, principal, or local butcher for help in obtaining a roll), have each group roll out a piece equal to the total height of the group's members, allowing approximately six inches overlap per student.

When the groups have finished measuring and cutting their roll pieces, ask them to work together to trace an outline of each group member on their paper, allowing approximately three inches between bodies. This is best done by having each student lie on his or her back, one at a time, while the others use pencils to trace an outline of the student. When the tracings are finished, the pencil lines can be highlighted with a dark felt marker. Students then use a felt marker to print their names vertically, with large block letters, on their body outlines.

Next, ask the groups to cluster around each student's outline, and decide positive statements or attributes that describe that student and start with each letter of the student's name. One of the group members then prints the word or words in their apprpriate place similar to the following example:

Example:

*K*ind

*A*thletic

*T*errific friend

*I*s a good soccer player

*E*asy to get along with

When the attributes have been printed for the letters in each student's name, the outlines are cut off from each group's roll and the students finish their outlines by coloring in their hair, eyes, clothing, etc. When the drawings are finished, each student cuts out his or her body following the outline. The bodies can be placed on each student's desk on the night of open house or parent-teacher conferences. They can also be displayed along the walls or in the hallway.

Variations

Depending on the size of the group and the time available, double sheets of paper can be used when cutting out each outline. The front and back sides can then be attached along the edge with a stapler, starting at the feet and working upward. Near the middle of the torso, students should stop stapling and start stuffing the outlines using discarded newspapers. They can then continue stapling and stuffing until a three-dimensional torso is created. Students might even bring clothes from home to dress their torsos. Placing the torsos in their appropriate desks during an open house can make quite an impression on students and their parents.

Source: Patricia Dzurick, early childhood teacher.

5.17

Who's Like Me?

Purpose

This strategy builds self-esteem and relatedness by providing students with an opportunity to learn which students in the classroom have interests similar to their own.

TARGET Areas

Task; Grouping

Grade Level

This strategy can be adapted to almost all grade levels and content areas.

Procedure

This activity is especially useful as an icebreaker with students who do not know each other well. Start by providing each student with a copy of the questionnaire in Figure 5.5 and a pen or pencil. Ask students to take a few minutes to compete column A of the worksheet. When they have finished, invite them to move around the room to find out who else in the class has the same answer. When they find a match, they should write that student's name in the corresponding space. Other matching students' names can be written on each blank.

After students have found matches for all or most of the items, you can go over each item and record the results for the class on the chalk-

FIGURE 5.5 Who's Like Me?

Directions: Write your answer to each question on the blank in Column A. Next, find other students in the class who enjoy the same things as you and write their names in the spaces in Column B.

	Column A	Column B
1. My favorite family pet		
2. The sport that I enjoy the most		
3. My favorite school subject		
4. My favorite food, excluding pizza		
5. My favorite color		
6. The month of my birthday		
7. The kinds of books that I enjoy		
8. My favorite TV show		
9. My favorite music group		
10. My most enjoyable hobby		
11. My favorite soda		
12. My favorite topping on pizza		
13. My favorite burger		
14. My favorite movie star		

board using a frequency table. Besides helping students identify similarities and differences with other class members, this part of the activity can be used to teach several math concepts, including addition, subtraction, fractions, percent, probability, and graphing.

Variations

Teachers can adapt the questions in Figure 5.5 to the age level and interests of their students. The worksheets can also be tailored to various aspects of a specific content area. Home economics teachers, for example, might ask questions that deal exclusively with student food preferences. Geography teachers might ask questions that focus on personal and family travel. English teachers might focus on books, poetry, magazines, or films.

Source: Sue Guzinski, high school learning disabilities teacher.

Wanted Posters

Purpose

This strategy enhances students' self-esteem and feelings of belonging by encouraging students to identify and share their unique contributions.

TARGET Areas

Task; Recognition

Grade Level

This strategy is most appropriate in elementary grades.

Procedure

Begin this activity by conducting a discussion of the types of individual characteristics that make students unique and special. Students can identify physical characteristics like color of hair, color of skin, birthmarks, freckles, color of eyes, or they can identify personal characteristics like smiles a lot, is friendly, likes to help others, or enjoys subtracting fractions.

Next, have each child draw a self-portrait on a 5 × 7 index card using felt markers, crayons, or colored pencils. Make an $8^{1}/_{2} \times 11$ inch Wanted Poster template similar to the one in Figure 5.6 and duplicate a copy of each student in the class. Ask each student to write or print his or her name on the name blank and to tape or glue their self-portrait to their Wanted Poster in the space provided. Then ask students to write

FIGURE 5.6   Wanted Posters

three unique characteristics about themselves on the lines underneath the self-portrait. Younger students may want to dictate their characteristics to the teacher as he or she writes them on the student's poster.

The teacher can display the posters in a corner or on a wall of the room under the title "We Are Wanted," or they can be placed in smaller groupings around the room.

Variations

With a small investment for film and processing, the teacher could bring in a camera and take a photograph of each student. The photographs could then be attached to the Wanted Posters. Posters could also be collected into a Big Book to be displayed in the class. Instead of creating Wanted Posters, the Big Book could be put together with drawings of the students doing something they enjoy doing well. The drawings could be mounted to larger sheets of paper followed by a sentence or two describing what the student is accomplishing. By placing a durable cover on the Big Book, students could take turns taking the book home to share with their parents.

Source: Linda Henika, elementary school teacher.

226

5.19

Family Book

Purpose

This strategy enhances self-esteem by encouraging students to investigate their nationality, heritage, and family traditions. Through this process, they should learn to value their own uniqueness and to appreciate the diversity of student backgrounds in the class.

TARGET Areas

Task; Recognition

Grade Level

This strategy is especially useful in elementary school.

Procedure

At the beginning of the school year, inform the class that each student will be expected to construct a family book that describes their family's nationality and background. Books should be approximately eight to ten pages in length and might follow a format similar to the following:

Cover Page—A decorated cover that includes the student's name, grade, school, and date.

Page 1—My family. This page should include a drawing or picture of the child's family. When children have two families, which is often the case in divorces, they can include both.

Page 2—My house. This page should include the student's address or addresses and phone numbers. It should also include a drawing or a photograph of the student's home.

Page 3—Celebrations. This page should include drawings or photographs of the various holidays, traditions, and cultural events that the child's family celebrates.

Page 4—Having fun. This page can include examples of what the family does for enjoyment during their free time.

Page 5—Food. This page can include drawings and recipes of the favorite foods that members of the family enjoy making.

Page 6—Talents and hobbies. This page should include drawings or pictures of family members who have special talents or hobbies.

Page 7—Work. This page should include drawings of family members at work either outside the family or in the home. It might also include the weekly chores that students are expected to do.

Page 8—Ancestral Roots. This page can include maps or drawings of the states or countries where the child's ancestors were born or raised.

Students should be encouraged to invite all of their family members to contribute to the construction of the book. Photographs, magazine pictures, and the student's drawings may all be used to illustrate the book. The books can be laminated, bound, and shared with classmates. At the end of the school year, each child can take his or her book home as a keepsake.

Variations

Each week during the school year a different student can be selected to share his or her book with the rest of the class. A half-hour per week can be set aside for this purpose and the family members invited to the class either to listen to the student's presentation or to talk about the family's history and ancestral roots with the class. They can also share hobbies, occupations, or ethnic foods with the class. Some teachers may want to have students construct tagboard dolls that they can dress in ways that reflect the traditional clothing of the student's ancestors. These can be hung in a mobile that will reflect the multicultural aspect of the class.

Source: Adapted by Renee Dassaw, elementary school teacher, from a presentation by Georgia Janza, reading specialist.

Accomplishment and Goal Sheet

Purpose

This strategy can build feelings of self-esteem by helping students focus on their personal accomplishments and the goals they wish to achieve.

TARGET Areas

Task; Recognition; Evaluation

Grade Level

This strategy can be used in all elementary grades.

Procedure

Begin this activity by discussing with your students the accomplishments and abilities that they have gained since infancy. Emphasize that people are constantly learning and that they usually feel pride when they have accomplished something that they were unable to do. Using yourself as an example, share a recent accomplishment for which you feel proud.

Give each student a piece of paper and have them fold it into four sections. Have them number the upper left section, 1; the upper right section, 2; the lower left section, 3; and the remaining section, 4. In each section of this accomplishment/goal sheet ask the class to draw a picture to answer each of the following unfinished statements (you will find it useful to write them on the chalkboard or on a transparency):

1. One thing I can do that I'm proud of is . . .
2. One thing I can do now that I couldn't do last year is . . .
3. Something I can't do now, but I can probably do next year is . . .
4. Something I can't do now, but I can probably do in five years is . . .

To model goal setting and the pride of accomplishment, it is important that the teacher complete an accomplishment/goal sheet with the students. When everyone has finished, ask the students to sit in a circle and share their pictures and responses with the group. The interaction will help others consider accomplishments and goals that they may have overlooked.

After all students have had an opportunity to share their accomplishment/goal sheets, they can be taken home and shared with parents, siblings, or relatives. You might want to attach a letter asking parents to discuss their own accomplishments and goals with their son or daughter.

Variations

Students, and teachers for that matter, might want to bring photographs or videos showing them accomplishing their activity or goal. Courageous teachers could bring in pictures of themselves when they were the age of their students. Both teachers and students might display their accomplishment/goal sheets and photos on a classroom wall or display board.

You might want to divide the activity into two parts: on the first day focus on the pride of accomplishment, and on the second day focus on short- and long-term goals. These can be displayed under the headings "Look What I Can Do Now" and "Look What I'm Going to Do."

Source: Adapted from Deanna Biermann-Schroeder, second grade teacher.

CHAPTER SIX

Strategies for Stimulating Student Involvement and Enjoyment with Learning

Psychiatrist William Glasser (1984; 1985) argues that the need for fun is basic to all human beings; people seek activities that provide physical, social, cognitive, or psychological pleasure. Intertwined with the need for fun is an individual's desire to laugh.

By definition, intrinsically motivating activities provide individuals with fun or enjoyment, although fun and enjoyment need not be limited to intrinsically motivating activities. Many activities undertaken for external goals can also satisfy similar needs. Many teachers, for example, find considerable enjoyment and fun in their jobs, although it seems likely that few would continue to teach if a paycheck did not accompany the activity. It seems reasonable to conclude that all students seek fun and enjoyment in school activities. When asked to describe the teachers in whose classes they are motivated to work their hardest, students invariably describe teachers who are enthusiastic about course content and find ways to make the learning interesting and enjoyable. Yet too often the word "enjoyable" has a bad reputation in schools. Apparently many educators believe that learning is supposed to be hard work, and if it's enjoyable, it cannot be serious or significant. This argument, however, is repeatedly contradicted by students' descriptions of classrooms in which they were highly motivated to do their best. It is in these classrooms that students are most willing to spend many hours learning content and meeting course objectives.

RECOMMENDATIONS FOR STIMULATING STUDENT INTEREST AND ENJOYMENT

1. *Find ways to get students actively involved in the learning process.* When students' minds or bodies are dynamically engaged in the construction of meaning and in the integration of ideas and skills, they become active participants in learning, rather than mere observers.

2. *Relate content objectives to student experiences.* Personal experiences are factually concrete and emotionally valuable. As a result, acknowledging student experiences and using them in the learning process stimulates intrinsic motivation.

3. *Assess students' interests, hobbies, and extracurricular activities.* If teachers are to relate content to student interests and experiences, they need to be knowledgeable about them.

4. *Occasionally present information and argue positions contrary to student assumptions.* When students are challenged by contrary ideas and opinions, they are stimulated to explore justifications, clarify facts, or alter beliefs—all processes that require active involvement and support intrinsic motivation.

5. *Support instruction with humor, personal experiences, incidental information, and anecdotes that represent the human characteristics of the content.* Students are highly receptive to the personal and humorous aspects of content since they help relate the material more directly to their own emotions and lives.

6. *Use divergent questions and brainstorming activities to stimulate active involvement.* Questions without right or wrong answers encourage creative thinking and stimulate intrinsic involvement and risk-taking.

7. *Vary instructional activities while maintaining curricular focus and structure.* By implementing a variety of activities and approaches, teachers can help students look forward to the unexpected challenges and stimulation offered by each class.

8. *Support spontaneity when it reinforces student academic interest.* Teachers should be ready to occasionally stray from a lesson plan when student interest is sparked by a topic not directly included in the lesson.

9. *By trying to monitor vocal delivery, gestures, body movement eye contact, and facial expression, teachers can evaluate the degree of enthusiasm conveyed in their teaching.* Attitudes toward learning are caught rather than taught, and students cannot catch a positive and enthusiastic learning attitude from dull, boring, and negative teachers.

10. *Instructional objectives should be reviewed and redefined to ensure that teachers recognize their value and are committed to ensuring that all students attain them.* Teachers need to value and be committed to what they are teaching if they hope to stimulate student interest and involvement in learning it.

6.1

Switch Day

Purpose

This strategy builds student interest and involvement, and enables students to experience variety in their school day.

TARGET Areas

Task; Authority; Recognition

Grade Level

This strategy can be adapted to upper elementary, middle, and high school.

Procedure

This strategy allows students to take over the roles of various school personnel for one day. In preparation for Switch Day, the teacher surveys all members of the school staff and support personnel to identify those willing to help a student take their role for a day. The teacher compiles a list of the staff volunteers and then discusses with the students the various skills that might be necessary to perform each role. After discussing the skills required, the teacher asks students if they would be willing to take one of these jobs for a day and to indicate their first, second, and third choices. Since several students may want the same job, selection is often a delicate process. The teacher may want to consult with the cooperating adult, but once minimum skills are satisfied, a lottery may be the fairest way to decide assignments.

Students assigned to roles should make an appointment with the staff member to discuss what will be expected of them on Switch Day, to learn any special skills that may be required, or to receive information about any lessons, meals, or special events that they need to plan. If necessary, follow-up meetings should be scheduled.

On Switch Day, students are called by their formal names and are required to dress appropriately for their roles, i.e., professional clothing for the principal's role, secretary's position, or teaching duties, uniforms (when possible) if replacing custodial staff, and hairnets and gloves as required for kitchen staff.

When the day begins, students report to their assigned positions and take over as much of the job as possible—depending on the situation, age, and skill level of the student; safety; and legal requirements. At the end of the day, the cooperating adult should be encouraged to provide the student with feedback regarding his or her performance.

If all or most of the students receive assignments, it may be useful to turn the classroom into a teacher's lounge for a day to allow the students rest and relaxation without disturbing the regular faculty. Efforts should be made to provide the same amenities available to the regular staff (soda, treats, television, comfortable seating, newspapers, etc.).

The following day, students should be encouraged to evaluate their success during the switch. What were their major difficulties and what part of the job did they enjoy the most? It is important to encourage students to write thank you notes to the cooperating adults.

Students seem to derive a great deal of enjoyment from the experience while having an opportunity to experience different career roles. Because of the wide variety of jobs available in most school settings, it should be possible for all students to experience success in this strategy.

Variations

If desired, the switch may be for just half a day, or even for a single period.

Source: Jeanne Koblewski and Melissa Zeman, elementary school teachers.

Function Machine

Purpose

This strategy can stimulate student interest and involvement in learning elementary mathematical functions by the use of a challenging but simple activity.

TARGET Areas

Task; Recognition

Grade Level

This strategy can be adapted to math classes at almost all grade levels.

Procedure

Start by making a copy of the function machine on the chalkboard, or using a permanent marker, on a transparency for use on an overhead projector (see Figure 6.1). Make up a simple mathematical equation on a sheet of paper, and without letting the class see it, ask a student to give you a number between 1 and 10 for the X value and write it in the X column of the function machine. Ask students to make a copy of the function machine in their notebooks, and when they have solved the function rule to write it above the X and Y columns. Using the previously deter-

FIGURE 6.1   The Function Machine

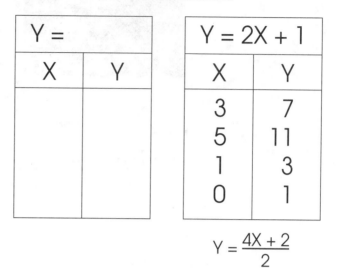

Y =	
X	Y

Y = 2X + 1	
X	Y
3	7
5	11
1	3
0	1

$$Y = \frac{4X + 2}{2}$$

mined equation, compute the Y value in your head or on a piece of scratch paper and write the value in the Y column.

Ask a different student for another number for the X column; write the corresponding Y value in the appropriate column. Those that discover the function rule will be raising their hands and will want to supply the Y value for the next X value. To avoid creating a competitive environment that discourages slower-learning students, invite those who have uncovered the rule to list other variations of the function. When all students have discovered the role, write the function on the top line of the function machine. Then ask students to share the variations to the function that they have discovered (you may want to write these on the chalkboard or transparency). With younger students, the functions can be very simple (e. g., $Y = X + 2$), while advanced algebra students can use calculators to baffle each other with tougher functions (e. g., $Y = \sin X$).

Variations

Depending on their previous experience with mathematical notation, elementary students might want to substitute "$f(X)$" for "Y" in their functions.

Source: Sally Yakel, math and study skills teacher.

Rhythm Pizza

Purpose

This strategy builds interest and involvement while helping students relate the fractional value of musical notes with a tangible illustration.

TARGET Areas

Task; Grouping; Evaluation

Grade Level

This strategy is most useful for middle and upper elementary grades.

Procedure

The class is divided into groups of three or four students. Each group gets a "pizza pan" (see materials list), a packet of "pizza slices," and a recording sheet. The groups are instructed to place various combinations of the pizza slices on their plate to arrive at a complete "pizza." The notes on the pieces are then transcribed onto the group's recording sheet in measures of 4/4. Notes should be transcribed in as many different combinations as possible (see example in Figure 6.2).

Once a pizza has been noted in all possible combinations, the group can assemble a new pizza with a different combination of notes. The notes

FIGURE 6.2   Rhythm Pizza

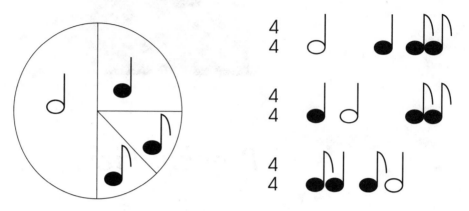

of this new pizza should then be transcribed to the recording sheet using all possible combinations.

When the students appear to have exhausted all of the possible combinations, the teacher ends the activity by asking each group to count the total number of measures that they have produced. The grand total for the class can be determined, and the tally sheets can be displayed on the bulletin board.

Materials

Each group will be required to have the following items:

- Paper plate with the following inscription, "Pizza Pan—one measure in 4/4 time"
- Two half-circle plates with a half note drawn on each
- Four quarter-circle plates with a quarter note drawn on each
- Eight eighth-circle plates with an eighth note drawn on each
- Sixteen sixteenth-circle plates with a sixteenth note drawn on each (a smaller number can be used)
- A lined sheet of paper to record each combination of notes

Variations

Each group could be asked to play their measures or could combine their measures into rhythm compositions during follow-up sessions.

Source: Linda Ruesink, elementary music teacher.

238

Animal Fact or Fiction

Purpose

This strategy is designed to stimulate student interest and enjoyment with learning. It also promotes independent research skills that build student autonomy and self-determination.

TARGET Areas

Task; Authority; Grouping

Grade Level

Although a second grade example is used, this strategy can be adapted to almost all grade levels and content areas.

Procedure

The teacher begins by reading the story "Animal Fact and Fiction" by Semour Simon from the second grade reader *Going Places* (Simon, 1993). The story is written in a way that allows the teacher to pose a statement about a particular animal and then ask the students if they think the statement is fact or fiction. (It may be useful to have students write the words "fact" or "fiction" on separate 3 × 5 cards and then hold up what they think is the appropriate card for each statement.) Sample statements might include: Ostriches bury their heads in the sand, dogs talk with their tails, and porcupines shoot their quills.

After students have exhausted the statements from this story, provide them with an assortment of books about animals (your school librarian should be a useful resource). Encourage students to read about an animal that interests them and to identify at least three factual statements about the animal. They should then construct three fictitious statements about the animal that their classmates might believe true. They might also want to draw a picture of the animal or select one from a book that they can share with the class. Some class time can be allocated to this project, and students can be encouraged to continue their research at home.

On an assigned date, give each student an opportunity to describe their animal to the class, show their drawing or picture, and then present their fact or fiction statements asking the class to vote with their 3×5 cards. A record of correct or incorrect votes can be tallied. Students might want to present their projects to other classes and the activity could culminate by placing all the drawings and statements in the class's own *Animal Fact and Fiction* book that could be displayed in the classroom or school library.

Variations

This activity makes a useful cooperative learning activity with each group selecting a particular animal and each group member compiling fact or fiction statements.

Source: Bonnie Kovelan-Hansen, elementary school teacher.

Orienteering

Purpose

This strategy is designed to stimulate student interest and involvement with learning. It also develops a sense of relatedness and positive interdependence among class members.

TARGET Areas

Task; Grouping; Time

Grade Level

This strategy can be adapted for grades four through twelve, but it is particularly suited to middle school where students are studying outdoor education, map reading, ecology, or natural sciences.

Procedure

Before class begins, the teacher uses a good-quality compass to mark off a five-leg orienteering course on school property. The five points should be specific landmarks (trees, stumps, poles) that are reasonable distances from surrounding objects.

The teacher introduces the class to the skill of orienteering by explaining the characteristics and uses of a compass. The class is then split

241

into groups of five students, and one member of each group comes to the front of the room to receive first-hand instruction in the use of the compass. The other students can arrange to perform complementary outdoor activities like tree measuring and mapping, bird-watching, litter pickup, and wildlife sketching.

Each group is then given an opportunity to complete the orienteering course. The first group member uses the compass to maintain a bearing as he or she walks off the required number of paces to the first mark (other group members follow behind). The first student then teaches another student how to use the compass to lead the group during the second leg of the course. As each mark is achieved, a group recorder makes a drawing of the orienteering course, clearly identifying each mark. After each group member finishes the course, they complete their drawing and return to the classroom so that another group can begin the course. If a group fails to identify a mark, they are asked to repeat the process to find their mistake after all the groups have had their first chance. One group can be randomly selected to pace out a different orienteering course for the teacher to complete.

Variations

The teacher may want to have all groups work on the course at the same time. In this case, each group could start at a different location with its own set of bearings.

A variation that younger students enjoy is to place small cards, not readily visible, near the base of each mark on the course. When the students are successful in locating the mark, the cards can instruct them to "Do ten jumping jacks" or "Howl like a wolf" before they go on to the next mark.

Source: Adapted by Katy Grogan, middle school English teacher; Row, K., Gilchrist, S., & Borneman, D. (1993). *One bird—two habitats: A curriculum unit for middle schools.* Madison, WI: Wisconsin Department of Natural Resources.

Anticipation Guide

Purpose

This strategy builds student curiosity and involvement by encouraging students to use their prior knowledge to make predictions about the content they are studying.

TARGET Areas

Task; Authority; Evaluation

Grade Level

This strategy can be adapted to almost all grade levels and content areas.

Procedure

This strategy uses an anticipation guide to build student involvement in text reading. The guide is composed of from three to five statements that either challenge or support students' prior knowledge and beliefs about the content to be studied. As students contemplate the anticipation guide statements, they develop an intrinsic purpose to read the text selection to determine the validity of their prior knowledge.

The following example demonstrates an anticipation guide for a middle school science lesson about lightning (Wham, 1988). Students are asked to read the following five statements about lightning and to identify those they believe are true.

1. Lightning never strikes twice in the same place.
2. It is safe to talk on the phone during an electrical storm.
3. During a storm, you are safer in a car than in a boat.
4. It is important to turn off electrical appliances during a storm.
5. Thunder is the sound made by the sudden expansion of heated air.

The teacher then conducts a discussion about lightning based on the students' personal knowledge of the topic. It is important that the teacher avoid confirming or refuting the students' opinions about lightning. All opinions are legitimate until the students have had an opportunity to read the text to validate their knowledge.

The following guidelines are useful for constructing anticipation guides (Readence, Bean, & Baldwin, 1981):

1. The teacher examines the text material on the topic to determine what major ideas to emphasize.
2. The teacher constructs three to five statements that challenge or support student opinions regarding key concepts. The teacher can stimulate curiosity by selecting statements for which most students have opinions but little factual information.
3. Statements can be presented using an overhead or chalkboard. Students should work independently to decide their agreement or disagreement before the group discussion.
4. During the group discussion, the teacher should encourage students to share their opinions and reasons rather than simply agreeing or disagreeing with the statements.

Variations

This activity can easily be adapted to cooperative learning groups. Each group can try to seek consensus regarding the guide statements and results can be compared with other groups.

A second discussion can be conducted after students have completed the text reading. They might identify any changes in their opinions that resulted from information presented in the text, or they might identify specific passages from the text that support or refute their previous beliefs. Students can also be encouraged to examine additional resources that might offer other information.

Source: Wham, M. A. (1988, Spring). Three strategies for content area teachers. *Illinois Reading Council Journal, 16*(1), 52–55; and Readence, J. E., Bean, T. W., & Baldwin, R. S. (1981). *Content reading: An integrated approach.* Dubuque, IA: Kendall/Hunt.

Know the Author

Purpose

This strategy can stimulate student interest in reading a variety of literature by introducing them to authors and their works. In addition, it can support student autonomy by promoting decision-making and personal evaluation skills.

TARGET Areas

Task; Authority; Evaluation

Grade Level

This strategy is especially useful in upper elementary and middle school; it can be adapted to high school literature classes.

Procedure

Select a book new to the class and find as much information as you can about the book's author. Begin by introducing the group to the author in one of two ways. First, if you have a good relationship with your class and you are willing to risk acting out of character, role play being the author and introduce yourself to the class. Talk about your background and share any interesting information that you have discovered in your research about the author. Describe other stories that you (the author) may have written as you lead up to the current work.

Holding up the book, tell the class why you wrote it. You may need to take a bit of poetic license as you extrapolate from the book's theme. Then introduce the class to the main characters of the book and their relationship to the story. Do this in an animated style as you try to build the students' interest in your story. You may choose to read one or two short segments from the book in order to build curiosity about the story, being careful not to reveal information that might undermine the suspense.

An alternative to role playing is to describe the author and his or her background. You can then introduce the book from the author's point of view without using first person.

Variations

Teachers can pique student interest by telling them that they will have a special visitor to their class on the day planned for the book introduction. If you are willing, you may want to dress in costume to further dramatize this activity.

Students especially enjoy dressing up and playing the role of author when they report on a special book that they have read. When the teacher models this approach beforehand, students seem more comfortable with role playing and provide a more thorough description of the characters and the story.

Source: Peggy Jo Maurer, media specialist.

Curious Questions

Purpose

This strategy is useful for building student interest and involvement in a new unit. It can also enhance feelings of competence in all students.

TARGET Areas

Task

Grade Level

This strategy can be adapted to almost all grade levels and content areas.

Procedure

Before the opening day of a new year, semester, or unit, the teacher writes out a series of questions (one for each student) related to the specific unit or general course content. The questions should be specific and factual, and written on self-adhesive stickers. Depending on the grade level and content area, examples might be: How many people live in the United States? Australia? Alaska? Wisconsin? France? and so forth. Who was the twenty-seventh president of the United States? What is the average number of scales on a sunfish? How many different notes are on the standard musical scale? Who were the two major explorers of central Australia?

On the day of the activity, the teacher places a question on each student's back as he or she enters the classroom. Each question is numbered, and each student is provided with the number but not the question. Students then move around the room and read each other's questions. Without mentioning the question, they then provide the student with the best answer they can. All students carry a sheet of paper to record the answers they have been given.

The teacher tells students that it is their responsibility to record an answer to their unknown question from every other class member. When students finish gathering their answers, they are instructed to review their answers and to write what they think is their question at the bottom of their paper. When everyone has completed this task, they remove the tag from their back and compare the question with their guess.

The teacher can now lead a discussion of the topic by asking each student to read their question and answers, and to share the reasons that they used to guess their question. The teacher can then provide the correct answer to the question before moving to another student.

Variations

This strategy can be a useful icebreaking activity by using general trivia questions or factual questions that relate to school, community, or state. Depending on the maturity and reaction of the class, the teacher may choose to use this strategy to begin several units throughout the year.

Source: Suggested by Ann Trow, elementary school teacher, Nancy Berkas, middle school math teacher, and Family Science, University of California–Berkeley.

What's the Score?

Purpose

This strategy is designed to build interest and involvement in writing. By making it a group activity, it can also support a sense of belonging and relatedness.

TARGET Areas

Task; Recognition; Grouping

Grade Level

This strategy is useful with middle and high school students.

Procedure

This strategy can be done individually or in small groups. The teacher asks students to select a game or sport that they are familiar with and that they can use to show the directions for scoring. Tell students that their goal is to write the steps required for keeping score or for playing. The teacher may want to read or duplicate the example in Figure 6.3 that describes the procedure for scoring of the first two frames in bowling.

Encourage students to be as specific and as detailed as necessary to completely describe the scoring procedure or game directions. Provide

FIGURE 6.3 How to Score the First Two Frames of Bowling

Each player rolls a large ball down a long strip of waxed wooden boards called a "lane" in order to knock over as many of the wooden pins at the end of the lane as possible.

First Frame—Ball One

If. . .

—the player aims poorly and the ball falls off the lane into the black trough, it is called a "gutter ball." Record a zero inside the little box inside the first square on the score sheet. The player then rolls the ball again.

—the player knocks over some of the pins, count the pins and write the number inside the little box inside the first square on the score sheet. The player then rolls the ball again.

—the player knocks over all the pins, it is called a "strike." Put an X inside the little box inside the first square on the score sheet. The player then sits down and must wait until the next frame to bowl again.

—the player crosses the little line on the floor at the beginning of the lane, called a "foul line," it is called a "foul." Record a zero inside the little box inside the first square on the score sheet. The player then rolls the ball again.

First Frame—Ball Two

If. . .

—the bowler got a strike on the first ball, he does not get a second ball; he has to sit down and wait for all the other players to bowl their second ball of this frame.

—after the second ball some of the pins are still standing, then put the number knocked down inside the second little box inside the first square on the score sheet. Add the first and second little boxes; place this total inside the square below these little boxes.

—the bowler knocks down all the remaining pins, put a slash into the second little box inside the first square on the score sheet. This is called a "spare," and the bowler must now wait for the remaining players to finish this frame.

Second Frame—Ball One

If. . .

—the bowler did not knock down all the pins in the first frame, count the number of pins and place it in the first small square of the second frame. The player rolls the ball again.

—the bowler recorded a spare in the first frame, add the number of pins knocked down, add ten, and put the total inside the first square of the score sheet. The player rolls the ball again.

—the bowler recorded a strike in the first frame, do not record anything inside the little boxes. The player rolls the ball again.

—the player gets a strike, place an X in the first little square of the second frame. The bowler must wait for the next frame to bowl again.

FIGURE 6.3 *Continued*

Second Frame—Ball Two

If. . .

—the bowler got a strike in the first frame and knocks down all the pins, add the number of pins from the second frame, put a slash in the second square of the second frame, and place twenty in the large box of the first frame.

—the bowler knocks down all the remaining pins, place a slash in the second square of the second frame.

—some pins are still standing, place the number knocked down in the second little square of the second frame. Add the first and second little squares of the second frame, add this total to the number of pins in the first frame, and put the number in the big square of the second frame.

students with class time to complete the assignment and then ask students or groups of students to read their directions to the rest of the class. The teacher can then conduct a discussion of how directions are used and how students feel about reading directions.

Variations

This activity lends itself to almost any logical or problem-solving application. Teachers of students in lower grades might use this strategy for writing the directions to solve subtraction or division problems. Some students might want to use this strategy to create the directions to their own games.

Source: Mark Stone, assistant professor of computer studies.

Expanding a Model

Purpose

This strategy builds student interest and involvement in the operations of an internal combustion engine. It also reinforces technical vocabulary while helping students visualize the interrelationships among the various components of an internal combustion engine.

TARGET Areas

Task; Grouping

Grade Level

This strategy is demonstrated with a middle school science example, but it can be adapted to almost all grade levels and content areas.

Procedure

In this example, the teacher obtains two copies of a poster or diagram of the operations of an internal combustion engine. Many science or physics texts provide these diagrams, or teachers of automotive or small engine repair classes at local vocational schools can recommend sources for posters that detail the components and operations of internal combustion engines. With one copy of the rectangular poster or diagram, divide the narrower side into three equal parts and the longer side into five equal parts. Next, draw parallel lines between the parts creating a 3 × 5 grid and dividing the poster or diagram into fifteen sections of equal size. With a scissors, cut the poster or diagram into the fifteen sections and distribute one section to each student or pair of students. To adjust for larger or smaller classes, you can vary the size of the grid and the number of sections.

Give each student or pair of students their section of the poster or diagram and an 18 × 18 inch piece of poster board. Provide students with pencils and markers and ask them to reproduce their smaller section by expanding it to the full limits of the larger poster board. Students will need to work with those who have bordering sections to ensure that their lines join at the appropriate places and there is room to label the components in their section appropriately. The second copy of the poster or diagram can be kept on display in the classroom to help students judge the relationship between their section and those that border it.

When all parts of the diagram are completed, the class will have a poster mesuring $4^1/2$ feet by $7^1/2$ feet. Move back some desks in the classroom and ask the students to tape the new poster to the floor. The new and expanded poster can be used to help students visualize how the engine works. Volunteers, for example, can pretend to be droplets of fuel and as they walk through the path of the fuel they can demonstrate or explain what happens to them at the various stages of combustion. Others can play the role of the pistons or valves and demonstrate what happens to them during or after combustion. If the classroom is large enough, the poster can be transferred to a wall where it can be used as a teaching aid throughout the unit.

Variations

The process of expanding models can get students actively involved in almost any content area. In biology, for example, diagrams of frogs or worms can be expanded; in history, diagrams of battlefields or maps of states or regions can be expanded; in math, expansion of three-dimensional geometric shapes can help students become actively involved in learning. Groups of three or more students can be used with more complicated posters or diagrams.

Source: Adapted from Stephen Werner, high school vocational education teacher.

The Farmer's Dilemma

Purpose

This strategy builds student interest and involvement while supporting students' problem-solving skills.

TARGET Areas

Task; Grouping

Grade Level

This strategy can be adapted to almost all grade levels and content areas.

Procedure

Divide the class into groups of four with each group member playing the role of either the farmer, his or her dog, a rabbit, or a bag of feed. These roles can be randomly assigned. If one, two, or three students remain after dividing the class into groups of four, have these students pair up with a farmer from another group.

Read the following story to the class (a dramatic tone builds suspense):

There once was a farmer who lived near a river. After an exceptionally wet spring and several days of torrential rain, the river was ready to flood. It was time, the farmer thought, to move his belongings to higher ground across the river. The farmer was a good swimmer and could manage to carry either his dog, rabbit, or bag of feed with him as he swam across the river. He was unable, however, to carry more than one possession at a time and would have to make three trips. As he decided which possession to take first, he realized that he couldn't leave the rabbit and the bag of feed together because the rabbit was a bit of a glutton and would eat it all. He also realized that he could not leave the dog and rabbit together because the dog did not especially like the rabbit and would eat him if he had the chance. Your task is to help the farmer solve his dilemma.

Solution:

The farmer carries the rabbit across first and leaves the bag of feed and the dog together. He then returns to take the bag of feed to the other side. Since he cannot leave the rabbit and the feed together, he brings the rabbit with him as he returns for the dog. He then leaves the rabbit at the starting point and takes the dog to the other side. He returns to take the rabbit across for the second time.

Encourage each group to work independently to solve the dilemma. If a group member has previously encountered the problem and solution, ask the student to refrain from giving the answer so that others can have an opportunity to solve the problem for themselves. After most groups have solved the dilemma, ask the group that was first to discover the solution to demonstrate the correct procedure in front of the class. You may also find it useful to conduct a class discussion of the factors that either helped or hindered each group's task.

Variations

Although it may be possible to have the groups compete against one another to find the solution, the dilemma generates enough interest that it would be superfluous to create competition among the groups. In many situations finding a solution to a complicated problem is a reward—we don't need to use extrinsic incentives to control the process.

Source: Unknown.

Wordsplash

Purpose

This creative and enjoyable prereading strategy is useful for building student interest and involvement in reading.

TARGET Areas

Task; Authority; Grouping

Grade Level

This strategy can be adapted to almost all grade levels and content areas.

Procedure

A wordsplash is a collection of key terms or concepts selected from an article, book chapter, lecture, presentation, or audiovisual that students are about to read, hear, or see. The selected words are "splashed" at angles on an overhead transparency or poster. Figure 6.4 provides a wordsplash for the following selection:

Iguana Farms—Wave of the Future?

One of the biggest sources of income in many Latin American countries is beef cattle. Since they require a large amount of grazing land, raising

FIGURE 6.4 Wordsplash for: Iguana Farms—Wave of the Future

deforestation

chicken

Costa Rica

Panama

dull-witted

96% mortality rate

domesticate

52 acres

40

five years

2.5 acres

50 cents per pound

6.5 pounds

styrofoam ice chests

drainage pipe

Stan Rand

beef cattle often leads to large-scale deforestation. In Costa Rica and Panama a group of researchers worked to find practical alternatives that would provide food and income without ruining forests. They came up with iguanas.

"They are ugly, they look prehistoric, and the thought of eating them is somewhat repulsive," Ira Rubinoff, director of the Smithsonian Tropical Research Institute, says of green iguanas. And most North Americans would probably agree. But in Latin America, iguanas have been considered good eating for thousands of years. Slow, dull-witted, and heavy with white meat that tastes something like chicken, these six-foot lizards have always fallen prey to hunters. It stands to reason researchers figured seven years ago, that iguanas would make ideal livestock. An average of 52 acres of rain forest is cut down each minute worldwide, largely because of the cattle industry's need for pasture land. But if tree-dwelling iguanas could be domesticated and raised in great numbers, they might provide meat to feed their owners (or to be sold for 50 cents-a-pound in the marketplace), and leave the trees in place.

Stan Rand, the resident iguana expert, felt that with a little tinkering he could devise an iguana-egg incubators that, combined with predator control, would bring down the 96 percent mortality rate of iguana eggs. Indeed, the iguana research project (with Dagmar Werner at the helm) managed to thoroughly domesticate the animal in five years, though some thought it would take one hundred.

The practical intuitive approach needed to apply research results to the rain forest proved to be the researchers' forte. Using supplies that local farmers could easily afford, they virtually eliminated juvenile mortality among iguanas. First they transformed a drainage pipe into a nest; then they turned soil-filled styrofoam ice chests into incubators. Miraculously, the iguanas caught on to both systems right away. The hatchlings were nurtured in cages until the age of seven months and, when ready to face the dangers of the wild, were released into a forest range dotted with feeding stations. Because female iguanas can lay up to 40 eggs at a time, they were soon reproducing furiously.

The researchers estimate that a community using their methods can now raise 100 iguanas a year, at 6.5 pounds each, in 2.5 acres of forrest—more meat per acre than many Latin American cattle ranches produce. The villagers are absolutely enthused about seeing the iguanas multiply and are planting trees like mad for new farms. Nobody burns trees anymore.[1]

Students are then asked to generate complete statements that predict how the splashed terms are related to the topic. The class can be divided into small groups to work on this activity, and a group recorder can keep a list of each group's statements. When the small groups have finished, have the recorder from each group read the group's predictions to the class.

Next, present the class with the reading material, lecture, or audiovisual presentation on the identified topic. After the class has read the material or listened to the presentation, encourage each group to discuss their predictions and to modify their statements considering their new information.

Variations

After students are familiar with this strategy, they can create their own wordsplashes. Used in this manner, the strategy encourages students to summarize the most important information from a reading or presentation.

Source: [1]Excerpted from Bilger, B. (June, 1989). "Beyond Beef." *Earthwatch*. Reprinted with permission from the publisher. Figure 6.4 is taken from Bruce Wellman (1993). Wordsplash is adapted from the work of Dorsey Hamond, Jon Saphier, and Bruce Wellman. Suggested by Connie Amann, elementary teacher.

Roundtable Rap

Purpose

This strategy can build interest and involvement in language arts skills while supporting group relatedness.

TARGET Areas

Task; Grouping

Grade Level

This strategy is most useful in elementary classrooms but the roundtable procedure can be adapted to almost all grade levels and content areas.

Procedure

Divide the class into groups of approximately four students. Prepare a list of topics related to the unit of study and select a key word for each topic. Write each topic and key word on a slip of paper, making sure to have at least as many topics and key words as student groups. Place the slips of paper in a box or hat and allow each group to randomly select one topic and key word.

After each group has selected a topic, encourage the group members to generate as many words as possible that relate to the chosen topic and rhyme with the key word. The roundtable procedure can be used to ensure that each group member has an opportunity to contribute to this process. This is accomplished by passing a sheet of paper and a pencil around the group with each person taking a turn to add a rhyming word to the list while the others in the group remain quiet. If a student cannot think of a word to add to the list, he or she may pass the sheet of paper after waiting fifteen seconds. The paper continues to go from student to student until all members have exhausted their repertoire of words.

Once the list of rhyming words has been generated, the roundtable procedure can again be used to generate a list of phrases that use each rhyming word and relate to the group's topic. Next, students within each group work together to organize the phrases into a rap song that makes sense and tells a story about the topic. Rap music can be played in the background to help establish a beat. ("Rap Hits," from Pocket Songs, MMO Music Group, Inc., 50 S. Buckhout St., Irvington, NY 10533, provides rap music without words.) Groups can be encouraged to practice the song on their own and then present their song to the class.

Round Table Rap Examples

Topic: autumn
Rhyming word: fall

Rap:
Paul is at the mall,
He is way too tall.
Or could he be too small?
The season now is fall.
The baby now can crawl
To the awesome wall.
The older Mr. Hall
Tossed him a brand new ball.
Raking the leaves in the fall,
Doing your chores now that is all!

Topic: autumn
Rhyming word: cat

Rap:
I saw a black cat sitting on a mat,
The night was spooky as the rat scared Pat.

A pumpkin fat fell off and went splat.
The witch's hat went flat when I sat.
A costumed brat was kissing a rat,
A big fat cat flew with the witch's hat.
Down I sat tripping on the doormat,
Trick or treat, now you can't beat that!

Topic: autumn
Rhyming word: ghost

Rap:
I saw a really cool ghost,
Who seemed to be eating toast.
At the party I ate the most,
Later I had a pot roast.
I went to visit the party host,
He lived down by the nearby coast.
I hate to brag, but I must boast,
I get my news from the Evening Post.

Student's in Mrs. Hill's fourth-grade class at Levi Lennard Elementary School, Evansville, WI demonstrate a "Roundtable Rap"

Variations

Depending on the age of the class and the content area, students may choose their own rhyming key word once a topic has been selected. Making a videotape of group presentations can increase student interest and provides a product to be shared with other classes or parents. Groups can also be encouraged to select a rap group name and to create signs or images to enhance their performance. Roundtable Raps can be organized around social issues or can be used to present findings from scientific research. They also can be used to demonstrate the power of advertising and propaganda.

Source: Betty Hill, elementary school teacher.

6.14

"15"

Purpose

In trying to use every minute of class time productively, this quick little game builds interest and involvement at the start of a class as roll is being taken, as a closing activity while waiting for a bell, or during those notorious dead times during transitions.

TARGET Areas

Task; Grouping; Time

Grade Level

This strategy is particularly useful in middle and high school math classes, but can be used at other grade levels and content areas.

Procedure

This activity is played with partners, and it seems to work best when students are free to choose their partners (the teacher may want to help shy students find partners). The game is played using a sheet of paper and the numbers 1 through 9. The players take turns selecting one number at a time until one player wins by having any three numbers total 15. Once a number is chosen, it cannot be used again. The game works easiest if the students write their selected numbers in side-by-side columns so that each student can see what numbers have been chosen.

Figure 6.5 provides an example of the game of 15. Player A begins by choosing the number 7 and writing it in his or her column. Player B decides to choose number 8 and writes it in the remaining column. Player A next chooses a 2, which means that player B needs to choose a 6 in order to block player A (7 + 2 + 6 = 15). Player A selects 1 to block player B (8 + 6 + 1 = 15). Player B, however, takes 4 which means that player A loses because there are three numbers remaining (9, 3 and 5), and two (3 and 5) will produce a win for B (8 + 4 + 3 and 6 + 4 + 5).

After students have played "15" several times, encourage them to try to figure out a pattern to the game. Some students will discover that the game is similar to tic-tac-toe, and if they memorize the pattern, they will do better than a student that is just choosing randomly. The pattern is:

2	9	4
7	5	3
6	1	8

Variations

Instead of the numbers 1 through 9, students can use the words HOT, TANK, TIED, FORM, HEAR, BRIM, WOES, WASP, and SHIP. The game is similar, but all the words should be written on the board, and the winner is the first person to pick three words that have the same letter in common. Again, the words distribute themselves into the following tic-tac-toe format:

HOTE	FORM	WOES
TANK	HEAR	WASP
TIED	BRIM	SHIP

Source: Bill Dehn, high school math teacher.

FIGURE 6.5   "15"

Player A	Player B
7	8
2	6
1	4
9, 3, or 5	9, 3, or 5

Pen Pal Picnic

Purpose

This strategy is useful to stimulate student interest and enjoyment in writing

TARGET Areas

Task; Grouping

Grade Level

This strategy is appropriate for most elementary grades.

Procedure

This strategy requires the teacher to contact a colleague teaching at the same grade level in a school located in another section of the city or in a surrounding community. The two teachers then establish pen pal arrangements between their two classrooms. Random selection is used to match students in the two classrooms, and when class sizes differ, some students will eagerly volunteer for two pen pals.

After assigning pen pals, the teachers can decide which class will send the first letter. These introductory letters can include a photograph of the author and a description of the author's family, pets, friends, favorite sports, music, books, or other interests. Letters are collected and mailed in a large envelope; students will anxiously await the arrival of the return package.

It is useful to establish a schedule to exchange letters every three or four weeks. Students can compare many aspects of their personal lives and can exchange information about their schools and teachers. They can also include samples of poems, artwork, and stories they have written. Questions like, "have you learned cursive yet?" and "How far are you in multiplication now?" and "What is the name of your reading book?" are commonly asked.

The culminating activity for this strategy is a joint picnic for the two classes near the end of the school year. This can be held in a centrally located park with parent volunteers used to provide transportation and treats. Students can then exchange home addresses and write to each other during the summer. Although it is easier to phone their new friends, teachers can encourage students to avoid this temptation so that they can continue to work on improving their writing skills over the summer.

Variations

Pen pal letters can be mailed individually rather than as a whole class, allowing some students to write more often. Younger students might enjoy an artwork exchange rather than letters. Teachers might also use "big brother" and "big sister" pen pals by matching classes separated by a year or two. Older students can be encouraged to serve as positive role models for the younger students who will be looking up to them.

Source: Linda R. Johnson, Jeanne Ste. Marie, and Debbie Oswalt, elementary school teachers.

Going Fishing

Purpose

This strategy builds interest and involvement in reviewing addition and subtraction facts.

TARGET Areas

Task; Authority; Recognition

Grade Level

This strategy is best suited for kindergarten through second grade.

Procedure

Using a template similar to the one in Figure 6.6, cut out about twenty fish from heavy construction paper. Laminating the fish will ensure that they last longer. Write one addition or subtraction problem on one side of the fish. Decorate the other side with eyes and gills, and glue a paper clip or nail to the middle of the fish. Spread the fish on the floor, problem-side down, in a small area of the classroom. Next, make a fishing pole from a stick and string, attaching a small horseshoe magnet to the end of the line.

Ask the class to pretend that they are about to go on a fishing trip. Before they leave for the fishing pond, they may want to make sailor hats to protect their heads from the sun. The teacher can illustrate this process

FIGURE 6.6   Going Fishing

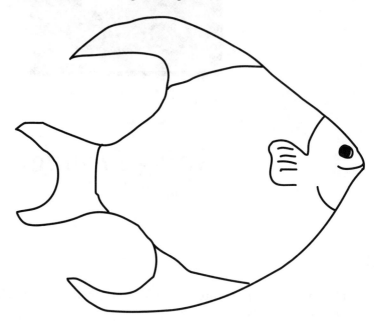

(see Figure 6.7) by handing out a sheet of newspaper to each child and showing how to fold the paper to create a sailor hat. (With very young children, the teacher may want to make the hats ahead of time and simply distribute one to each student.)

With donned hats, the children should quietly sneak up to the fishing pond and sit in a circle on the floor surrounding the fish. It is important that they be very quiet so as not to scare the fish away. Let one student at a time fish for a problem. When they have landed the fish, the teacher should ask what they caught. At this point, the student should read the problem aloud, such as, "5 + 2 = ?" and then solve it. If students get the answer right, they should give the fish to the teacher and pass the pole to the student on their left. If the problem is answered wrong, the fish is thrown back into the pond to be caught by another student. The fish should be upside down as so not to expose the problem, and the teacher may want to mix the fish in with the others while the students close their eyes for a couple of seconds. The game ends when all the fish have been caught.

Variations

It is probably best to go fishing in small groups of four or five students to avoid boredom while students are waiting for a turn. Besides simple

FIGURE 6.7 Fishing Hat

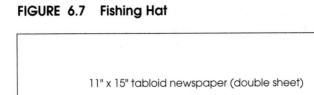

11" x 15" tabloid newspaper (double sheet)

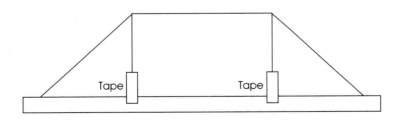

Tape   Tape

math problems, the teacher can tape different problems to the backs of the fish that relate to colors, shapes, letters, basic sight words, days of the week, months of the year, or similar short-answer review questions.

Source: Suggested by Lisa Gottschalk, first grade teacher.

The Human Adding Machine

Purpose

This strategy builds student curiosity and interest as they watch their teacher mentally add a long list of four-digit numbers. This impressive feat will surprise students and will get them actively involved in learning the strategy so they can impress others with their mental prowess.

TARGET Areas

Task; Recognition

Grade Level

This strategy can be adapted to almost all grade levels and content areas.

Procedure

This strategy uses a simple but impressive addition procedure that will allow the teacher to add a long list of three-, four-, or even five-digit numbers quickly, without adding separate columns, and from right to left rather than the usual left to right procedure.

Begin by asking students to shout out four-digit numbers as you write them on the chalkboard. For example, taking any first number, assume that it is 6537. Write this number on the chalkboard:

6537

Next, take any second number, for example, 7431. Now you have:

6537
7431

At this point, you include your own number on the list. It is the number that makes the four digits in the previous number each total nine. In this case, it is the number 2568:

6537
7431
2568

You now take another number from the class. Assume they give you 6952. Adding it to the list gives you the following:

6537
7431
2568
6952

Now add 3047 to the list since it makes each digit in the previous number total nine:

6537
7431
2568
6952
3047

Again, take another number from the class. For our example, assume that it is 7211. Add this to the list and the number that makes each digit total nine:

6537
7431
2568
6952

3047

7211

2788

You can continue the procedure, but this is enough to demonstrate the addition procedure. First count the number of pairs that total nine. In this case, there are three pairs: 7431 and 2568; 6952 and 3047; 7211 and 2788.

The number of pairs, three in this example, becomes the first digit of your answer. Next, subtract the number of nine-pairs from the first number given to you, and that number now becomes the last four digits of your answer. Here the answer is 36,534:

6537

7431

2568

6952

3047

7211

2788

36,534 (the number of pairs [3], followed by the first number minus the number of pairs [6537 – 3] = 36,534)

A bit of showmanship while doing the quick addition will make your feat even more impressive. Ask a student to check your addition with a calculator. If you have carefully followed the above procedure, your answer will be correct.

As you gain experience demonstrating this procedure, you can use five- or six-digit numbers and make the list as long as you like, as long as you match all numbers except the first with a corresponding number that creates a nine-pair.

Note: If the first, first and second, or first, second, and third digits of a four-digit number start with nine, then you must use only a one-, two-, or three-digit number to create a nine-pair.

Source: Taught to the author by Les Baumgardner, special education teacher.

Talking Chips

Purpose

This strategy builds a sense of group cohesiveness and relatedness by encouraging all students to contribute equally to a group discussion. It also prevents shy students from being overwhelmed by the more vocal students.

TARGET Areas

Task; Recognition; Grouping; Time

Grade Level

This strategy can be adapted to almost all grade levels and content areas.

Procedure

This strategy is useful any time students are divided into small groups to discuss issues relating to course content. Each student is given a poker chip or similar object at the beginning of the class or school year. They can be encouraged to write their name on the chip with a marker and keep it in their desk for use throughout the year. If students move to different classrooms throughout each day, the teacher can keep the chips in a box on his or her desk. Each student can then take a chip from the box during those periods when this activity will be used.

The guideline for this activity is that students can contribute information or ideas to their group's discussion only after they have placed their talking chip in the center of the table. After taking their turn, they are prevented from sharing additional information or opinions until all members of the group have used their talking chips. When the last person has placed his or her chip in the center and spoken, group members can retrieve their chips and begin the process again, each relinquishing a talking chip when they want to contribute and waiting until all chips are used before retrieving it.

When first using this strategy, teachers will find that students will often be thinking more about when to use their talking chips than about what others are saying. However, after they get used to waiting for others to contribute before adding additional thoughts, they will concentrate more on the contributions of others and will wait to make more thoughtful contributions of their own.

Variations

By giving students two or three talking chips at the start of a discussion, group members can follow up on the ideas of others without having to wait until all have used their chips. This can contribute to a more natural discussion while still preventing one or two students from dominating.

Teachers can use this strategy when conducting large group discussions. If a few students seem to dominate, the teacher can simply remind students to make sure that others have an opportunity to use their "talking chips" before they make additional contributions. Although the physical chips may not be present, students will learn to give others a chance to contribute before they make additional comments.

Popcornology

Purpose

This strategy uses student interest and familiarity with popcorn to springboard into many different academic content areas and skills.

TARGET Areas

Task

Grade Level

This strategy is most appropriate for elementary and middle school.

Procedure

With many students, the shortest route to the brain is through the stomach. Stimulating student interest and enjoyment is easy with food—it's a natural motivator. From toddler to adult, most are willing to get actively involved in any activity when the final product is eating. In such cases, food is not used as a bribe, but as a culmination to the learning activity.

One of children's most popular foods is popcorn. Figure 6.8 lists some interesting and little-known facts about this enjoyable food product. The following list provides suggestions for using the study of popcorn to meet academic objects in several content areas:

FIGURE 6.8 Popcorny Facts

- American colonists often ate popcorn for breakfast mixed with fruit, milk, and sugar. Fixed this way, popcorn tastes somewhat like puffed cereal.

- Two tablespoons of unpopped popcorn costs between three and eight cents and make a quart of popped corn.

- More popcorn per capita is eaten in the United States than in any other country in the world.

- Popcorn that is too dry will not pop. Placing the kernels in a jar with two table-spoons of water for a few days can take care of this problem.

- Nebraska, Indiana, and Iowa grow most of the world's popcorn.

- Native Americans often strung popped corn to make necklaces and other jewelry.

- Native Americans often make soup with popcorn.

- More popcorn was served in movie theaters during *Star Wars* than any other movie.

- In 1519, the explorer Cortez saw Aztec statues decorated with popcorn.

- Anthropologists found 5,600-year-old popcorn in the New Mexico Bat Caves.

Language Arts

- Write commercials for a new brand of popcorn, selecting a creative and descriptive name for their product.
- Write a story about "The Popcorn That Wouldn't Stop Poping" or "The Kernel That Wouldn't Pop."
- Describe your favorite "popcorn place."
- Write "Legends and Tall Tales" about popcorn.
- Use the word "popcorn" to provide an example of short and long "o" words. Have the class make a list of short "o" words.

Science

- Make predictions about the absorption of water by popcorn. Fill a glass with popcorn kernels. Add water to the top and place an index card over the glass. Have the children predict what will happen in twenty-four hours. (Popcorn will absorb so much water that the popcorn will overflow.)
- Soak kernels in water. Place with wet tissue in a zip-lock bag. Make a record of your observations regarding the germination of the seeds.

- Have children make hypotheses about the question, "What makes popcorn pop?" (When popcorn is heated, water inside the kernel expands and eventually causes popcorn to "explode.")
- Place an air popper in the center of the floor and have the class measure and graph the distance that each kernel lands from the popper.

Math

- Compare cost per serving of snack foods.
- Measure volume of popcorn before and after popping.
- Weigh and compare popcorn before and after popping.
- Measure circumference of largest kernel.
- Record the number of unpopped kernels.
- Graph information that leads to conclusions regarding the quality of different brands of popcorns.

Social Studies

- Research the role of popcorn in the lives of Native Americans and early colonists.
- Research the size and importance of the American popcorn industry.
- Trace the life of a kernel of popcorn, from planting to popping.
- Make a time line of historical events in the history of popcorn.

Resources

The Popcorn Institute, 401 N. Michigan Ave., Chicago, IL 60611-4267.

Source: Patricia Bantz, elementary school teacher.

Floor Puzzles

Purpose

This strategy is used to foster group relatedness and cooperation. It also generates enthusiasm and interest in problem solving.

TARGET Areas

Task; Grouping

Grade Level

This strategy is most appropriate for preschool and early elementary levels.

Procedure

Take a large piece of tagboard and paint a background using two or three different colors (with two colors, paint half one color and the other half a different color; with three colors, paint one-third in each color). Using a pencil and ruler, divide the painted tagboard into as many squares as there are students in the class. Each student is assigned a square and asked to draw a self-portrait in the space. Since only two or three students can work on their self-portraits at a time, this strategy should be combined with other activities.

When all students have completed their self-portraits, cover the tag-board with clear contact paper and use a large, sharp scissors to cut it into twenty to twenty-five different-sized and -shaped pieces. Give each child two or three pieces of the puzzle. Explain to the children that they are going to work together to construct a large class portrait from their pieces. Suggest to the children that they may help each other by pointing out where a piece will fit, or by suggesting helpful strategies such as "turn the piece over" or "move the round part this way." It is important, however, to emphasize that each child should be the only one to place his or her pieces into the puzzle.

Initially, it may be necessary to remind students not to touch the pieces of others. As students have more experience working on the floor puzzle, there will be more and clearer verbal suggestions and an increase in team effort.

Variations

Several variations are possible. The teacher might take a photograph of the class with a standard 35 mm camera. The convert the photograph into a poster using one of many companies that advertise in the back pages of popular magainzes. Paste the poster to the tagboard and proceed as above.

To simplify drawing the self-portraits, children can draw the pictures on smaller pieces of paper that can then be cut out and glued to the tag-board.

Source: Suggested by Carol Flora, primary school teacher.

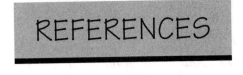

REFERENCES

ALBERT, L. (1989). *A teachers's guide to cooperative discipline.* Circle Pines, MN: American Guidance Services.

AMES, C. (1990). Motivation: What teachers need to know. *Teachers College Record, 91,* 409–421.

AMES, C., & ARCHER, J. (1988). Achievement goals in the classroom: Student learning strategies and motivation processes. *Journal of Educational Psychology, 80,* 260–267.

BERMAN, S., & LaFARGE, P. (1993). *Promising practices in teaching social responsibility.* Albany: State University of New York Press.

BINGHAM, M., EDMONDSON, J., & STRYKER, S. (1994). *Challenges: A young man's journal for self-awareness and personal planning.* Santa Barbara, CA: Advocacy Press.

CLASEN, D. R., & CLASEN, R. E. (1993). Synectics in the classroom. In P. J. HILLMANN, D. R. CLASEN, & R. E. CLASEN (Eds.), *Teaching for thinking: Creativity in the classroom* (3rd ed.). Madison, WI: University of Wisconsin–Madison Educational Extension Programs.

CONNELL, J. P., & RYAN, R. M. (1984). A developmental theory of motivation in the classroom. *Teacher Education Quarterly, 4,* 64–77.

DECI, E. L., & RYAN, R. M. (1985). *Intrinsic motivation and self-determination in human behavior.* New York: Plenum Press.

DEWEY, J. (1913). *Interest and effort in education.* Carbondale: Southern Illinois Press.

DREIKURS, R. & SOLTZ, V. (1964). *Children: The Challenge.* New York: Hawthorn Books.

DREIKURS, R. (1968). *Psychology in the classroom* (2nd ed.). New York: Harper & Row.

DREIKURS, R., GRUNWALD, B., & PEPPER, F. (1982). *Maintaining sanity in the classroom: Classroom management techniques* (2nd ed.). New York: Harper & Row.

EPSTEIN, J. L. (1988). Effective schools or effective students: Dealing with diversity. In R. HASKINS & D. MacRAE (Eds.), *Policies for America's public schools: Teacher equity indicators.* Norwood, NJ: Ablex.

EPSTEIN, J. L. (1989). Family structures and student motivation: A developmental perspective. In C. AMES & R. AMES (Eds.), *Research on Motivation in Education* (Vol. 3). New York: Academic Press.

FLEISCHMAN, P. (1988). *Joyful noise: Poems in two voices.* New York: Harper & Row.

FLEISCHMAN, P. (1988). *I am Phoenix.* New York: Harper & Row.

FRANK, L. (1988). *Adventures in the classroom, a stress challenge curriculum.* Madison, WI: Madison Metropolitan School District.

FREIDENBURG, E. Z. (1959). *The vanishing adolescent.* New York: Dell.

GLASSER, W. (1984). *Take effective control of your life.* New York: Harper & Row.

GLASSER, W. (1985). *Control theory in the classroom.* New York: Harper & Row.

GLASSER, W. (1990). *The quality school.* New York: Harper & Row.

HERMAN, J., ASCHBACHER, P., & WINTERS, L. (1992). *A practical guide to alternative assessment.* Alexandria, VA: Association for Supervision and Curriculum Development.

JONES, V., & JONES, L. (1990). *Comprehensive classroom management* (3rd ed.). Boston: Allyn and Bacon.

KOHN, A. (1991). Group grade grubbing versus cooperative learning. *Educational Leadership, 48*(5), 83–87.

KOHN, A. (1993). *Punished by rewards.* Boston: Houghton Mifflin.

LEPPER, M., & GREENE, D. (Eds.). (1978). *The hidden costs of reward: New perspectives on the psychology of human motivation.* New York: John Wiley & Sons.

MARZANO, R., PICKERING, D., & McTIGHE, J. (1993). *Assessing student outcomes.* Alexandria, VA: Association for Supervision and Curriculum Development.

OAKES, J. (1988). Tracking: Can schools take a different route? *NEA Today, 6*(6), 41–47.

ORENSTEIN, P. (1994). *School girls: Young women, self-esteem, and the confidence gap.* New York: Doubleday.

PFEIFFER, W. J., & JONES, J. E. (Eds.). (1969). *A handbook of structured experiences for human relations training* (Vol. 1). Iowa City, IA: University Associates Press.

PFEIFFER, W. J., & JONES, J. E. (Eds.). (1974). *A handbook of structured experiences for human relations training* (Vol. 3). Iowa City, IA: University Associates Press.

RAFFINI, J. P. (1980). *Discipline: Negotiating conflicts with today's kids.* Englewood Cliffs, NJ: Prentice-Hall, Inc.

RAFFINI, J. P. (1993). *Winners without losers: Structures and strategies for increasing student motivation to learn.* Boston: Allyn and Bacon.

READENCE, J. E., BEAN, T. W., & BALDWIN, R. S. (1981). *Content reading: An integrated approach.* Dubuque, IA: Kendall/Hunt.

REASONER, R. (1982). *Building self-esteem: A comprehensive program.* Palo Alto: Consulting Psychologists Press.

ROW, K., GILCHRIST, S., & BORNEMAN, D. (1993). *One bird—two habitats: A curriculum unit for middle schools.* Madison, WI: Wisconsin Department of Natural Resources.

SCHMIDT, F. (1993). *Peacemaking skills for little kids* (2nd ed.). Peace Works Series. Miami Beach: Peace Education Foundation.

SCHRUMPF, F., CRAWFORD, D., & USADEL, H. C. (1991). *Peer mediation: Conflict resolution in schools.* Champaign, IL: Research Press.

SIMON, S. (1993). Animal fact and fiction. In *Going places (2nd grade reader).* New York: Silver Burdett & Ginn.

SPADY, W. G. (1988). Organizing for results: The basis of authentic restructing and reform. *Educational Leadership, 46*(2), 4–8.

UNGARETTI, L. (1988, September). Ugly ducklings. *Learning88,* supplement.

WELLMAN, B. (1993). *Increasing student science achievement using outstanding cooperative learning and critical thinking techniques.* Bellevue, WA: Bureau of Education & Research.

WHAM, M. A. (1988 Spring). Three strategies for content area teachers. *Illinois Reading Council Journal, 16*(1), 52–55.

WHITE, R. W. (1959). Motivation reconsidered: The concept of competence. *Psychological Review, 66,* 297–333.

WIGGINS, G. (1993). *Assessing student performace.* San Francisco: Jossey-Bass.

WLODKOWSKI, R. J. (1978). *Motivation and teaching: A practical guide.* Washington, DC: National Education Association.

INDEX

Accomplishment and Goal Sheet, 229–230
Acheson, T., 62
Adlerian psychology, 7
Adolescence and self-esteem 10–11
Advanced organizer, 50–51
Alternative assessment, 111–112
Amann, C., 258
Ames, C., 15
Anderson, B., 43
Animal Fact or Fiction, 239–240
Anticipation Guide, 243–244
Apathy, 5
Appreciation Web, 128–129
Assertive, Aggressive, or Passive?, 151–154
Authority structure, 13–14
Autonomy
    need for, 3–5
    recommendations for enhancing, 17–18
    strategies for enhancing, 19–67

Bailey, G., 22
Baldwin, R., 244
Bantz, P., 278
Basler, J., 152
Baumgardner, L., 273
Baumgart, T., 30
Bean, T., 244
Beedle, H., 32, 94, 147
Belonging and relatedness
    need for, 7–9
    recommendations for enhancing, 121–122
    strategies for enhancing, 123–180
Berkas, H., 248
Biermann-Schroeder, D., 230
Big and Little Buddies, 142–143
Bilger, B., 258
Bingham, J., 154
Birthday Circle, 141
Borneman, D., 242
Brainstorming Bonanza, 130–131
Brandt, J., 161
Breen, D., 109
Bubolz, C., 60

Can You Top This?, 169–170
Care Cards, 216–217
Carroll, J., 175
Character and self-esteem, 10
Check It Out, 33–34
Choice, 6
Choices, importance of, 17
Choral Poetry, 81–82
Christianson, A., 131
Churchill, W., 186
Clasen, D. R., 98–99, 102
Clasen, R., 98–99, 102
Class Photo Album, 176–177
Coaching Choices, 61–62
Collins, J., 80
Competence
    need for, 5–7
    recommendations for enhancing, 68–69
    strategies for enhancing, 70–120
Conover, J., 159, 184
Construction of meaning, 12
Cooperation Dilemma, 123–125
Crossnumber Puzzle, 86–88
Curious Questions, 247–248

Daily Math Journal, 103–105
Dassaw, R., 226
Dehn, B., 264
Deichl, B., 57
Dewey, J., 12
Dreikurs, R., 7–9
Dzurick, P., 222

Edison, T., 186
Edmondson, J., 154
Einstein, A., 186
Eliminating Failure, 108–109
Ellington, Duke, 187
Enjoyment. See Involvement
Epstein, J., 12–16
Estimating Esquire, 75–76

Evaluation structure, 15
Expanding a Model, 252–253

Failure-avoidance behavior, 66
Family Book, 227–228
Feelings Chart, 58–60
"15", 263–264
Fit My Category, 106–107
Five Squares, 148–150
Fleischman, P., 82
Floating A, 27–28
Floor Puzzles, 279–280
Flora, C., 60, 280
Fun, need for, 11
Function Machine, 235–236

Gilchrist, S., 242
Glasser, W., 11, 231
Goal Books, 38–39
Goal Cards, 23–26
Going Fishing, 267–270
Gottschalk, L., 270
Grading Rubrics, 110–112
Graphic Note Taking, 77–78
Grogan, K., 74, 78, 82, 193, 242
Group Filmstrips, 160–161
Grouping structure, 14–15
Gumdrop Tower, 155–159
Gurholt, J., 64
Guzinski, S., 224

Hall, R., 85, 88
Halverson, K., 82
Hamond, D., 258
Henika, L., 226
Hill, B., 261–262
Hillmann, D., 102
Hintz, J., 120
Hohner, M., 164

Icebreakers, 140–141
Identity and self-esteem, 10
Iguana Farms, 256–258
Infomasters, 165–166
Intrinsic motivation
    components, 3–12
    defined, 3

Involvement and enjoyment
    need for, 11–12
    recommendations for enhancing, 231–232
    strategies for enhancing, 233–280
Isaacson, B., 28

Janza, G., 228
Johnson, L., 170, 266
Jones, J., 159
Jones, L., 46, 114, 149–150, 177, 219
Jones, V., 46, 114, 149–150, 177, 219

Kid Questions, 40–41
Kirk, K., 34
Kjelstrup, S., 190
Know the Author, 245–246
Know-Want-Learned Listing, 70–72
Koblewski, J., 46, 234
Kohn, A., 1–2
Koss, J., 92
Kovelan-Hansen, B., 240
Kreil, P., 180

Life Line, 194–195
Logan, J., 206, 212
Logical consequences, 4
Lucey, M., 129

Math Mind Reading, 83–85
Maurer, P. J., 246
McAuliffe, C., 186
Measuring the Motivational Climate, 126–127
Moorman, C., 117
Moss, A., 166, 204
Multicultural Celebrations, 167–168
My Me Book, 199–200

Name and Body Acrostic, 220–222
Name Bugs, 191–193
Newsroom, 21–22
Nicholls, J., 1
Norm-referenced evaluation, 15
Nuts and Bolts, 132–134

Oakes, C., 15
Orenstein, P., 206, 212
Orienteering, 241–242
Oswalt, D., 170, 266
O'Beirne, B., 202

Peacemakers, 52–53
Pen Pal Picnic, 265–266
Pfeiffer, L., 53, 200
Pfeiffer, W., 159
Piaget, J., 4
Pick Your Points, 31–32
Pinwheels, 162–164
Popcornology, 276–278
Prahl, P., 48–49
Punishment, 4, 8
Put-Ups, 188–190

Quality Checklist, 29–30

Random Acts of Kindness, 207–209
Random Grouping, 135–139
Readence, J., 244
Reasoner, R., 181
Reflective Participation for Everyone, 79–80
Relatedness. See Belonging
Resident Specialists, 218–219
Reward structure, 14
Rewards
    negative effects, 1–3
    used to control behavior, 4
Rhyming Names, 140
Rhythm Pizza, 237–238
Rohnke, K., 175
Rotar, J., 78
Round Tuits, 19–20
Roundtable Rap, 259–262
Rousch, S., 187
Ruesink, L., 238

Sallam, W., 107
Sanborn, P., 125
Santy, L., 143
Saphier, J., 258
Schoenbeck, L., 198
Sdano, R., 134
Seeing with the Mind's Eye, 89–90

Self-awareness and career choice, 35–37
Self-concept, 9
Self-determination. *See* Autonomy
Self-esteem
    need for, 9–11
    components, 9–10
    recommendations for enhancing, 183–231
    strategies for enhancing, 181–182
Self-Report Card, 44–46
Sentence Polishing, 42–43
Silent Solutions, 213–215
Similarity Wheels, 196–198
Simon, S., 239
Siodlarz, W., 105
Smith, C., 120
Social Studies Hot Seat, 47–49
Social interest, 7
Spady, W., 16
Ste. Marie, J., 170, 266
Sternad, P., 76
Stick-On Encouragers, 201–202
Stodala, M., 51
Stone, M., 251
Stranded, 171–175
Stryker, S., 154
Success Contract, 93–94
Super Squares, 178–180
Switch Day, 233–234
Synectics, 97–102

Talking Chips, 274–275
Target structures, 12–16
Task structure, 13
Teacher-Advisor Program, 65–67
Teichow, D., 109
The Gender Journey, 210–212
The One-Hour Book, 118–120
The Day You Were Born, 203–204
The Human Adding Machine, 271–273
The "I Can" Can, 113–114
The Death of "I Can't", 115–117
The Farmer's Dilemma, 254–255
The Minute Monologue, 141
The Unwritten Dialogue, 72–74
The Teaching Assistant, 91–92
Thome, D., 177
3-D Self-Portrait Box, 183–184
Through the Gender Looking Glass, 205–206
Tijerina, K., 177
Time structure, 16
Torrence, T., 39
Trapp, B., 71–72
Treasured Object, 141

Tropical Tribune, 144–147
Trow, A., 248

Ugly Ducklings, 185–187

Van Brocklin, S., 200
Voting with Your Feet, 63

Walsh, R., 202
Wanted Posters, 225–226
Wellman, B., 258
Wellness Awareness, 54–57
Werner, S., 253
Westmas, J, 143

Westra, L., 67, 120
Wham, M. A., 96, 243–244
What's the Score?, 249–251
White, R., 6
Who's Like Me?, 223–224
Wilson, W., 187
Wlodkowski, R., 11
Word Sort, 95–96
Wordsplash, 256–258

Yakel, S., 41, 236

Zeman, M., 23